KARATE INSIGHTS

Lessons for Life

BY RICK L. BREWER

DISCLAIMER:
Please note that the author and publisher of this book are NOT RESPONSIBLE in any manner whatsoever for any injury that may result from practicing the techniques and/or following the instructions given within. Since the physical activities described herein may be too strenuous in nature for some readers to engage in safely, it is essential that a physician be consulted prior to training.

First published in 2018 by Empire Books/AWP

© Copyright 2018 by Empire Books/AWP LLC. All rights reserved. No part of this publication may be reproduced or utilized in any form or by any means, electronic or mechanical, including photocopying, recording, or by any information storage and retrieval system, without prior written permission from Empire Books/AWP LLC.

Library of Congress Catalog Number:
ISBN-13: 978-1-949753-03-5

Empire Books/AWP LLC, P.O. Box 401788, Los Angeles, CA 90049

Library of Congress Cataloging-in-Publication Data
Names: Brewer, Rick (Karate instructor), author.
Title: Karate insights : lessons for life / by Rick Brewer.
Description: First edition. | Los Angeles, California : Empire Books, 2018.
Identifiers: LCCN 2018042810 | ISBN 9781949753035 (pbk. : alk. paper)
Subjects: LCSH: Karate--Philosophy. | Conduct of life.
Classification: LCC GV1114.3 .B73 2018 | DDC 796.815/3--dc23
LC record available at https://lccn.loc.gov/2018042810

Dedication

I dedicate this book to my lovely wife, Donna,
who helped make it all possible.

And I dedicate this book to my students,
past and present. I hope I can continue to inspire
and challenge them, as they have me.

Foreword

I AM DELIGHTED TO WRITE THIS FOREWORD to the work *Karate Insights,* not only because Sensei Rick L. Brewer has been a friend for many years, but also because I believe deeply in the educative value of all the philosophies and principles that he is addressing in this book. I believe that karate teachers at every level and stage of their career can enrich and strengthen their teaching by learning the budo concepts and training presented in this valuable work.

Over a long and fruitful career, Sensei Brewer has studied, explored and applied the philosophy and practice of budo through his classes and seminars around the world. He has conceptualized the intellectual foundations of these warrior's principles, elaborated a clear format to be understood, studied its patterns and taught them to other teachers and students.

Reading this book, you will find that good teachers are born, but they have to me "made" as well. Like the ancient samurai who knew that when facing a razor-sharp blade, physical skill would not suffice if the mind and the spirit were distracted, Sensei Brewer provides today with this work, the compelling evidence that a true karate-do philosophy can be taught and learned by teachers of all styles, but not without serious and sustained dedication. And what better way to strengthen the quality of karate teaching and learning in all our dojo?

I hope that this book will become a primer for teachers, coaches, educators, and professional karate trainers, helping them to learn, teach, and practice the true philosophy of the art of the empty hand.

--- JOSE M. FRAGUAS

Acknowledgements

I FEEL DEEP GRATITUDE for the inspiration of all my students and friends, and to the internationally famous karate masters like Senseis Osamu Ozawa, Hidetaka Nishiyama, Hirokazu Kanazawa, James Yabe, Stan Schmidt, Shojiro Sugiyama, Randall G. Hassell and many others who have touched my journey. They all helped me, little by little, for over fifty years, to write this work. I share many of their thoughts and many of my own. This is humbling, and easily keeps one with "the beginner's mind."

The seeds of motivation to research concepts in this book to obsession, lured me into traditional karate training over 50 years ago. Some, resulting from the need of overcoming bullies and bad guys, and yearning for empowerment to overcome fears and challenges. As a child I was a weakling, I suppose, with asthma, allergies, and a non-athletic frame; too puny to fight and too slow to run away. By pure luck, I met my strong-as-a-bull, kindhearted firefighter neighbor, who trained while stationed in post-World War II Japan, and who frequently smashed boards bare-handed to entertain the neighborhood kids. I was one pesty neighbor kid who would just not go away. I could never get enough.

I have been fortunate for the outstanding influences of my many colleagues, instructors, peers, and friends who've similarly chosen their own life-time karate path. There have been many. A special "thank you" to my friend and "partner-in-crime," Carl L. Hartter. Carl helped karate grow and prosper in our regional and national karate work. Together we worked hard to teach traditional Shotokan karate and founded organizational structures to help our students train, progress, and flourish in universities, high schools, commercial dojos and community programs, from children's programs up through, well, more "seasoned" adults of all ages. Carl has supported me and helped me raise my own bar.

I started teaching teenagers in the high school where I taught. Many of those still train to this day, are black belts, and are leaders wherever they are in the world. I was fortunate to teach all sorts of students, and I could not be more thankful for it --- especially to my most senior students, Ted Quinn and James Hartman, who started as awkward high school teens in the 1970s, and who are now superior established karate instructors, I give my admiration.

In those early days, my goal was to mold their teenage adolescent character using all the assets and power of traditional karate. This required quite a bundle of spirit training, with the lessons in citizenship and character building, from all the karate knowledge and technical skill sets I could muster. In the 1970s, I had what was one of only a handful of programs like it in the U.S. We had a Pekin Community High School Karate Club with a competitive team, and an accredited high school Board of Education approved karate course. I feel gratitude for landing in a school district with the vision to see how wonderful karate could be to shape the character and physical well-being of youth. It seemed to me quite parallel to Master Funakoshi's goals in his early Okinawan years, introducing karate into schools. I looked toward his example.

ACKNOWLEDGEMENTS

A product of that educational environment, James Hartman has been a fine police defensive tactics and firearms instructor who serves his community every day on the Peoria, Illinois Police Department. He has been my right-hand man in keeping classes running smoothly, week in and week out, year after year, in our Central Illinois Shotokan Karate Association. He is always a bundle of creative energy and action in all our karate classes, projects and challenges. He has been a great mentor and example for students young and old. From his police work, he brings applications of karate to the reality of the streets. He offers street-wise perspectives to our karate students and is obsessed with the potential usefulness of all things karate. Sharing his experiences with students brings relevance and a new sense of urgency that leaves them wide-eyed and motivated. He has an insatiable thirst for karate knowledge.

Out of that same quite lively group of original high school students came another real source of inspiration for us all, Ted Quinn. I could never have known that a decade later in Japan, he would be presented a winning kata award by the Secretary of Defense of Japan. He was my first student Shodan. I was guilty of "brainwashing" Quinn in high school with all my karate history lessons, samurai stories, and spirit-training pep talks. Training in Ebisu at the Hoitsugan dojo, the Japan Karate Association in Tokyo promoted him to Sandan. He joined the U.S. Air Force and spent over 12 years in Japan. Quinn competed with the Japanese on the Japanese Self-Defense Force team several years in All Japan Championships in the Budokan. He was a true ambassador of good will in Japan. Today, he teaches and mentors in our Central Illinois Shotokan Karate Association dojos, is a teaching assistant in the very high school where his karate began. His dedication to karate still inspires all.

Carl Hartter and I worked on many events with famous instructors like Osamu Ozawa, Hirokazu Kanazawa, Stan Schmidt, Randall Hassell, and the like. Those experiences afforded priceless learning opportunities for ourselves and all our students. Together we were able to forge an organizational model for traditional karate student development, from beginners to internationally certified black belts. It was through Carl's friendship, help and support for over 40 years that some of the more interesting events highlighted in this book transpired. If we were accused of trying to give our students no-frills, hardcore, old-fashioned Shotokan karate, we would plead guilty.

I vowed early on that I would not knowingly turn away a karate student because, due to hardship, they lacked the funds for classes. Consequently, karate organizational and community partnerships with not-for-profit community institutions have been wonderful, and I have been accused of practically giving karate away through these good relationships. The Pekin YWCA, Mapleton, Hollis Park District, Pekin Boys and Girls Club, and Peoria County, Kickapoo dojos, Community High Schools, and many other programs have offered our students excellent karate opportunities for decades, since 1975. The importance of community-based karate clubs and programs cannot be overstated. Karate-do and karate spirit-training are famous for citizenship and leadership building. What could be better for building and supporting productive citizens than the traditional character-building precepts of karate? What a wonderful way of developing outstanding future community members.

ACKNOWLEDGEMENTS

One of those outstanding community members is John Garls. He is a blackbelt and has taken it upon himself to take a few thousand photos over the years, many used in this book, and produce CDs and DVDs for our students and does volunteer invaluable technical assistance for our host facilities, and he is our first go-to man for helps when my PC takes off with a mind of its own when I write my columns, articles and books. And in our down-time, he and I enjoy precision target shooting with firearms, and he is a great shot, too! That, with his karate, technical IT knowledge and his marksmanship, make him a wonderful contributor to our dojos in front and behind the scenes, and he is a great friend.

I first read Sensei Randall G. Hassell's column, *"The Karate Spirit,"* in BLACK BELT MAGAZINE, back in the early days of my training and teaching. I remember thinking, *'This guy got it right. He thinks just like me! This is what real karate is supposed to be; our thinking, our reflection, and our "karate spirit" should be like this.'* This was why I started karate. More than just being tough, karate is cerebral. Karate is *budo*. I was thrilled to read every word, month after month, year after year. I just had to meet this guy some day!

In the 1980s I took my students to meet Randall Hassell and participate in one of his AJKA tournaments. There was an immediate good feeling, and my students enjoyed themselves. Our common goals were obvious. In the late 1980s, Carl Hartter and I merged our Central States Shotokan with the newly formed American JKA Karate Association (AJKA,) which later evolved into the American Shotokan Karate Alliance (ASKA). I tried to always be principle-driven like the teachings of Gichin Funakoshi. Carl and I have worked hard to follow karate paths that were ultimately student development-centered, in traditional karate way, providing the best pathways of karate instruction for our students using international standards. This has proven to be wonderfully beneficial formula for our students. Together with the help of thousands of students and scores of our instructors, we have kept our traditional karate organization healthy for fifty years.

I must sincerely thank Sensei Randall G. Hassell. He taught, inspired, and encouraged me tremendously --- to teach karate and to write about karate in my dozens of articles and for this book. In fact, my first karate article featured the adventures of my student, Ted Quinn, and his exciting years in Japan. Ted had written me letters of his experiences from the first person. It was as if I could see it all happening in my mind's eye, and I had a burning desire to write about it and share it with a larger audience. So, I took a deep breath and asked Sensei Hassell if he would be willing to give me some writing pointers and maybe edit my new rough draft. I was excited. He more than happily consented. When he gave back my manuscript, holy cow! It had so much red ink on it, it looked to be bleeding out. Sensei Randall Hassell was a superior instructor, an excellent task-master, a mentor, and a dear friend. He was a renowned traditional Shotokan Karate Master in the truest sense of the word.

I had some wonderful, unexpected encouragement in my early writing days that continues to this day. When I first started writing about hardcore traditional karate training, there was a quirky competition for the early martial arts hype with mystical secrets, "death touches," and so on. I was afraid magazine editors and publishers would not want traditional blood, sweat, and callouses karate articles. Out of the blue, I received a phone call from Jose Fraguas, who enthusiastically encouraged me to write even more articles about traditional karate; punching, kicking, sweating out on the dojo floor. This completely started a mentorship and friendship that I have highly valued for many years.

When teaching like-minded karate enthusiasts and students, the results are rewarding. But, "no man is an island." I appreciate the difficulties I caused my family with my karate obsessions. Growing up, my kids, Jeremiah and Jessica, thought it was just normal for everyone to have a dojo in their basement and makiwaras decorating the back yard. They thought it was "normal" for all fathers to "kiai!" using the punching post or doing techniques. I never understood why my daughter's high school friends didn't always come up to the door to pick her up with a courteous knock. "Dad," she told me, "They're afraid of you!" Who knew?

My family accepted my, to put it mildly, possible obsessions related to karate. Above all, I think my dear wife, Donna, has had to exercise more patience for over 40 years with me than any ten Zen monks. She has given me more encouragement, support, and sometimes first aid, than seems humanly possible. She has always brought me perspective and helped clear my vision. She knows as much about the karate ways as any black belt. For all the family affairs that were rescheduled, adjusted or postponed because of karate tests, clinics, tournaments, classes, and the like, I owe her, big time. I am so grateful for her kindness and understanding all these years. She is my partner and my rock. I appreciate her so much.

Preface

"Spirit training" is the multifaceted sum of essential components of karate-do that direct the intensity and implementation of all physical activity. The calm, disciplined, everyday-spirit outlined in the *Dojo Kun* and *20 Precepts* of Master Gichin Funakoshi, is meshed with the ever-aware, split-second, explosive, subconscious-directed actions that would nullify even the most ferocious animal. There is the peaceful spirit of disposition and conviction that Funakoshi stressed as the essence and necessity true karate-do. And there is Musashi's "void," the highest stage of karate-do described by Masatoshi Nakayama, where accumulated training is internalized to the extent that the martial artist can react with perfection, with no prior indication of danger, at any time or place. What all have in common is the dedicated and disciplined daily study of our conscious thought streams and subconscious mind, coupled with "internalized" karate skills… Or, the sum could be described as "Spirit Training." Webster's defines "spirit" as the "life-giving force," or the "animating component, or stimulant." All of that is inseparable from karate-do.

I have always encouraged my students to make karate become part of their lifestyle. The "karate lifestyle" can support a healthy, disciplined, inquisitive and well-adjusted human being. It combines the strengths of character from traditional karate-ethics updated with the preparations for the rapidly growing complexities of today's demands and challenges. Karate Spirit-Training supports strengths and fortifies weakness, stimulates growth and motivates. It is never old fashioned. In fact, its traditional elements are more usable, valuable, and relevant than ever. Used as a character-building, health and fitness, dependable source of positive energy and attitude development, it is incredibly empowering.

If you are a good karate teacher, you are a lifelong learner; always the "beginner's mind." Spirit training is about learning the tangible and the intangible. The top of the iceberg is obvious, but the true strength of what we see lies beneath. That is where we can always look for more to make sense of what we think we see. Our insights and studies here are rather comprehensive, very meaningful and quite powerful. Like all martial art studies, we look wide and deep. We learn from everyone, everything, and every experience. This book reflects that empowering process. It is meant to be an insightful lens of all that is easily over-looked, and to see what is too often missed.

Chapter 1

Introduction

OBSERVE AND MODEL YOUR KARATE SPIRIT after the life-force of the tiny green plant that, against all logic, grows up through the smallest unforgiving crack in solid rock-hard concrete in any sidewalk under foot. Respect and be in awe of the small, hundred-year-old pine tree rooted stubbornly to the solid granite mountain cliff; admire its tenacity. This is the *karate spirit*.

Webster's defines "spirit" as the "life-giving force," or the "animating component, or stimulant." We must, train this.

Karate spirit training has nothing to do with religion. It has everything to do with the life-force or animating components that cause us to move forward in karate working toward character-building, living peacefully, while building karate technique into our natural way of moving through our lives like a big cat. We learn to calmly meeting challenges as they come and living a karate lifestyle: karate-do. According to Master Masatoshi Nakayama, his teacher, Gichin Funakoshi, stressed that the most important side of karate training is "nurturing the sublime spirit, a spirit of humility" while at the same time developing the power to "destroy a ferocious wild animal with a single blow." In true karate, students must work toward perfecting "these two aspects: the one spiritual, the other physical."

Nakayama says in his *Best Karate Fundamentals*, that the spiritual aspects of karate training must play "a predominant role." According to Nakayama, "inflicting damage on an opponent with one blow of the fist or a single kick has, indeed been the objective of this ancient Okinawan martial art. But even the practitioners of old placed stronger emphasis on the spiritual side of the art than on the techniques."

Spirit in its simplest form can even be the state of mind that we are in daily, or mind forces we put into play when action is demanded by outside forces. Karate training is, by its very nature, interacting with extreme challenges. We usually think these are largely caused by aggressors or antagonistic influences trying to somehow do us in. "Spirit-training" in karate, helps us learn to use, focus, and magnify our own "life-giving force," and powerfully animated energy, simultaneously and explosively, with our applied karate technique. Even more important, however, is that karate spirit training strengthens our character and integrity, in order to point our compass in the right direction for personal growth as we weave through life's unpredictable and demanding challenges.

In our average, everyday, civilized, often pampered lifestyle, our very existence, our lives, are not routinely at stake. Exceptions, of course, are for those whose jobs have inherent life-threatening elements: first-responders like police, firefighters, emergency medical professions, military, etc., wherein proactive spirit training is needed. A karate lifestyle,

INTRODUCTION

with all its inherent training features, can help tremendously in many aspects of our lives on a daily basis.

My day job, my career as both a public high school Career and Technical Education teacher and administrator was extremely challenging. I taught many troubled teens for 35 years. It was my dedication to karate training that allowed me to accomplish goals, seemingly against the odds, of empowering young lives for the best, in an upstream environment. Karate spirit training was a powerful energy source to recharge my own batteries.

We often watch news about someone being victimized from an "it won't happen to me" or "ignorance is bliss" disposition as a default comfort zone. People start to learn karate for many reasons: fitness, self-defense, curiosity, to meet new people, and the like. This is all just fine if they have low to moderate expectations for surviving truly violent, life-threatening situations. Serious karate training, with spirit and technique inseparably meshed, is a truly effective weaponless solution to overcoming attack. Memorization of karate techniques is useful for minimum expectations. It is only the training of the body, mind, and the spirit combined, that is most highly effective in life and death dangers.

Spirit training, as described in this book, is the process of managing our intangible life forces with resolve. We supercharge our actions with extraordinary vigor to create the energy and inspiration needed to exceed the norm.

Traditional karate training is becoming passionately dedicated to perfecting something that can never be perfected. The motivation to continue comes from an inner drive that hungers to surpass all previous personal limits; even if only by the slightest increment.

Funakoshi said, "Karate is a lifetime endeavor; there are no limits." Now train and remember, "There are no limits."

The Case for Spirit Training

We are all safe and content, until the rules of civil behavior break down; and the wolves get hungry.

Karate-do is all about training both the mind and the body. In fact, Funakoshi's 20 Precepts clearly express that mental training is even more important than physical technique. The mind is the major generator of healthy vigor, an enthusiastic disposition, and it is the vehicle of subconsciously directed energies. This potentially powerful aspect of karate training is often neglected.

On the other hand, someone who has trained to cultivate both a strong mental spirit and high levels of technical training is a very dangerous person. The results are strikingly obvious. Honing mental skills and strengths, both conscious and subconscious, is "spirit training."

When opponents are of equal physical strength and skill, the one who is mentally stronger will usually win. And someone of lesser physical strength but with strong mental awareness, discipline, and tactical experience can beat a stronger opponent. Mental strength is somewhat abstract, maybe harder to grasp at first, but the results of its cultivation and application are immeasurable. Mental strength is "spirit strength" and requires regular and disciplined training, just as technical skill sets require regular and disciplined training.

Karate is more than just preparing for conflict. With correct karate training we avoid crisis if possible and strive to successfully cope with confrontational forces as required. Correct and thorough karate training is an exercise in how to be a better human being.

Through karate's spirit training, new patterns of thinking and behavior emerge from countless experiences on the dojo floor and through reflection and directed thinking. Martial art technique is the engine; spirit training is the raging fire in the furnace. The human being is changed forever.

Clear Thinking and Mental Power

Sometimes people think that spirit training and mental power are hocus pocus, smoke and mirrors, nonsense and silliness. This is unfortunate collateral damage from charlatans, video games, Hollywood CGI, and flagrant misrepresentations of karate presented to the public. Many misunderstandings have been attributed to martial arts promotion and marketing, especially with today's amazing quality of computer graphics (Hollywood style). For many who have dedicated their lives to their martial art this can be fun entertainment, or sometimes sad, bordering on ludicrous, especially if you love traditional karate-do (and have common sense.)

Compare someone performing karate just for novelty exercise, for "the burn," with someone demonstrating karate with disciplined high-spirited purpose, commitment, and clear-minded mental focus. You will quickly note a striking difference. A clearly focused mind is always the best conduit to direct high-spirited energy to attain quite remarkably energized results.

Understand that clear and correct thought is a powerful tool and affects all aspects of your life. Frequent benefits of karate training pop up in all quarters of day-to-day life. But you needn't just take my word for it; let's look around at the evidence.... here are some powerful words to inspire and motivate. Below are examples of "mere words" that are striking. They are food for thought, and can upend past paradigms to cause new ideas to flourish:

> *"Always remember: Your adversaries prefer your silence, apathy, and inaction. Be the consequence, not the victim."*
> --- ANTHONY COUCHENOUR

> *"Every time I put on my gi I am prepared to die! Understand?"*
> --- MASTER OSAMU OZAWA
> (looking me squarely in the eye…and I understood!)

> *"Live each day as though your hair were raging with fire!"*
> --- MIYAMOTO MUSASHI

> *"Happiness doesn't depend on who you are or what you have. It depends solely on what you think."*
> --- DALE CARNEGIE

> *"In all things, man must have a clear mind."*
> --- GICHIN FUNAKOSHI

Chapter 2

The Spirit of Authenticity

IN 1975 I STARTED A KARATE CLUB in the large public-school district of Pekin Community High School, in Central Illinois. I was beginning a challenging new career as a Career and Technical Education teacher. After four years of college at Illinois State University in Education, and continuous karate training, I spent time in naval officer flight training schools with marine drill instructors. I thought with all my education and additional military training, that teaching high school would be a breeze. Teaching teenagers and working in education proved to be a very challenging career "adventure" that I enjoyed immensely. I taught by day in the high school and taught karate at night. I was a teacher, a Career and Technical Education Department Chair, and was even for 14-years an elected School Board member in the district where my children attended school. And all the while, karate was my most energizing source.

After college, I was a black belt when I went into the military. Luckily, in the service I had met black belts from several karate styles, so I always had karate friends to train with. After my military service I was absolutely thrilled to dive into my teaching career. I had enjoyable internships, student teaching, and several years of karate teaching. I was ready to take my plunge into an education career.

Starting out in the high school teaching job was all set, but I was no longer near my familiar karate settings. Now I was on my own. With my new job and new people, I trained in private, in any spare room I could find after my school day was done. I found that karate channeled the nervous energy I had accumulated through the day to good use (Punching and kicking hard was very therapeutic!) and the "moving Zen" aspect of karate recharged my batteries to face the next day of teaching six consecutive hours of students with raging hormones. Soon my secret after school training hideout was discovered by a handful of students and faculty members. They were popping in and bugging me incessantly during the day with questions about karate. They would just not go away! Little by little, they started training with me and the numbers grew; their interest was insatiable

They slowly persuaded me to start an official school club. As they say, "The rest is history." In the early 1970s, an "official" karate club was a new concept in public high schools in the U.S., and to my knowledge was one of the first of its kind. Because of the outlandish rash of Hollywood martial art movies at that time and their often plotless violence, I had a public relations problem from the start. I knew that I had to educate the school, parents and the community on the proper virtues of Shotokan karate. I saw karate as a tremendous asset to the lives of confused adolescents, but most people were only familiar with the rush of violent karate movies.

Being a brand-new teacher in the school and with the crazy reputation karate was receiving, I tried to keep a low profile at first. We held regular 2-hour practices twice a week after school. I always emphasized the positive character-building aspects of traditional karate, proper karate student behaviors in class, and ways they should work on being good citizens in school, and at work, or at home. Of course, our workouts were pretty intensive as they progressed, but teenage minds are malleable, and their joints were flexible at that age. I was so surprised to find that the average 16-year old was in poor physical condition, but we soon took care of that! Positive feedback from parents was profound.

One morning, the school PA announcements said we would be having a half-hour karate demonstration in our gymnasium before lunch. The students were very excited about it and classroom control that morning was certainly strained. I knew nothing about it and we were the only karate club in our school. I was more than interested!

This would have been comical if it wasn't real. As we filed into the gym — over a thousand students and teachers — I saw a gentleman in all black attire with assorted colorful patches, with a shiny 4-foot katana and a very large collection of fruits and vegetables. I couldn't resist edging over and standing next to our principal. Our guest speaker said that he was going to show us all a "genuine karate-power show!" (Prompting me to wonder why the swords and fruit stand?) What? Then, he went on say that if we liked this karate demonstration, we should all come out to the big circus tent just out of town and see even more "karate stuff!" And after the "bigger karate show" that evening, he would have a "small church revival service" for everyone and pass the hat. (So much for the separation of church and state…nevermind.)

For the next 30 minutes the so-called "karate master" chopped a salad on stage. He then blind-folded himself and asked for student volunteers (This wasn't looking good for student safety, in my mind.) Then he put carrots in the mouths of the students and proceeded to chop them, one slice at a time, closer and closer to the unsuspecting noses. Next, our snake oil salesman karate expert, blindfold still in place, had students lie down while he placed melons (then working his way down to cucumbers) on their tender, trusting bellies. With a shout and a swing of the sword, he sliced and diced melons and cucumbers down to pickles on the giggling adolescents.

Admittedly, I was incensed in every fiber of my traditional karate, *art of the empty-hand* body. Remember that I stood next to the principal, my boss, headmaster of the building. I could only take so much, so I leaned over to his ear and said, "I'm so sorry this is happening because this is in no way karate of any kind. This is an unqualified clown show and it has nothing to do with real karate. Please come watch our club after school. My students and I will show you real karate. I promise."

Unfortunately, our "Musashi-wanna-be" continued slicing, doing his Vegamatic bit within millimeters of student flesh. I leaned over once again to my new boss and said, "Do you guys have lots of liability insurance, just in case?"

The law states that schools have the same responsibility that a parent would have over students. I don't think parents would have been thrilled watching this. I was sad to think a thousand students would go home raving about how the "karate master" chopped fruit and veggies with a sword. To me it was an example of a fraudulent misrepresentation, and a blatant lie, about the amazing power of traditional karate. I was both repulsed and motivated beyond repair!

Fast forward to Spring: I was relentless for our new karate club to give another and very different assembly, showing true authentic karate training. There were no "smoke and mirrors," just very high-spirited students showing authentic, traditional Shotokan karate. I took the microphone and stressed the wonderful karate spirit-training components that improve mind and character, and contribute to good educational processes and good citizenship-building. In other words, we just basically presented a true picture of our typical karate class.

We got wonderful reviews, the karate club flourished, and we even got the first accredited high school karate class by a unanimous school board vote. Differing from the world of charlatans, quality traditional Shotokan karate just sold itself. This was the correct method to introduce our high school students, faculty, and administration to good karate, its mental and physical benefits, and ways it could contribute to improve the lives of our students.

Chapter 3

Using This Book

THE PURPOSE OF THIS BOOK is to stimulate intellect and to strengthen emotions and motivation. It is to assist you in animating your own "life forces" at will: your karate spirit. Karate is the perfect medium to do this because proper spirit training is an essential element of all aspects of traditional karate-do. There is the spirit that is explosive and highly animated, and there is the spirit that is calm and contemplative. We can learn to use, control, and benefit from the wide range of types and levels. This book consists of strong inspiring statements, reflections, some points on my experiences, and many points from select karate masters who have been instructive and helpful in shaping the correct karate spirit for millions of students this past century.

To get the best out of this book, read a concept and reflect upon it for a while, then go back and read it again. You don't need to read in any particular order; read in the order that you feel helps you. Spirit-training is personal and requires us to internalize concepts deeply, even into the unconscious (subconscious) levels of the mind. This always requires serious practice in and out of the dojo and more. But make no attempt to memorize. Read and absorb the concepts in small bits. Work to allow ideas to soak into your understanding and into your intuition. Especially in your quiet times, when you can have some solace and hear your own thoughts, read an entry, lay the book down, and think about it. Many of the concepts are actually best for long-term attitude formation and paradigm shifts: "light bulb moments" bring a new way of seeing what has always been there, hidden in plain sight.

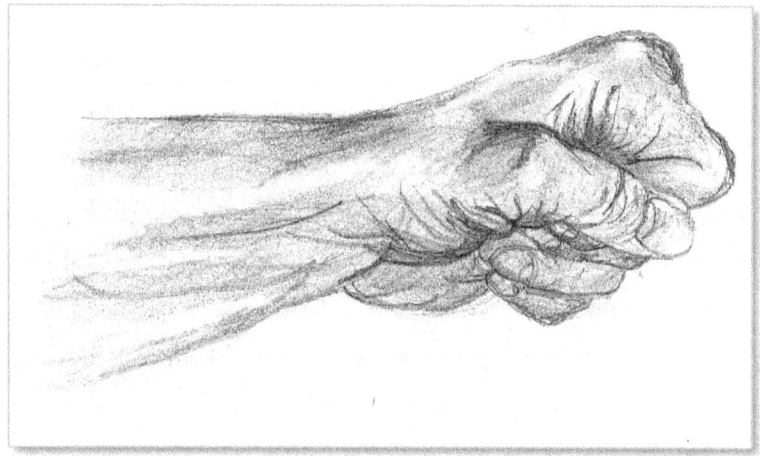

When possible, make selections of these concepts to use the next time you are on the dojo. Some are even utilized best, and experimented with, out on the floor, facing an opponent. You should probably try no more than one or two concepts at a time because otherwise you may forget them as soon as you take a stance. Please understand that thoughts used by warriors over millennia are not new. But, if you have never used the concept in your own training or thinking, it's like buying a pre-owned race car. It's new to you! It is always important to try to learn some small new thing from everything that we do. Be a life-long learner. That is why we must always maintain the "beginners mind."

As instructors, we ponder, practice, and make the best use of whatever we can to stimulate learning in our students and ourselves. As a karate teacher, if we are successful, we go further to figure out ways to pass methods and ideas along to our students in both concrete, and abstract ways. Try to perceive the applications of spirit and mental energy in your training and in your life. Never stop learning and trying to improve what is done and who we are. Oh, and one more thing...

> *"Do nothing that is of no value."*
> -- MYAMOTO MUSASHI

My ramblings from here on are to cause reflection, inspiration, maturity and growth. If applied and practiced with determination and serious contemplation, we can grow to attain higher skill-set levels, gain more in-depth and introspective appreciation and a deeper internalization and understanding of your martial art.

> *Do not over-think; do not judge;*
> *just learn, never stop, and never give up.*

Chapter 4

Spirit Training is Grounded in Reality

AT AN INITIAL FIRST GLANCE, the concept of "spirit training" seems to deal with the abstract, the invisible, but it absolutely does not. It is not hype or mysticism, but has very real purpose. It is, in fact, reality in the extreme, and its effects are highly detectable and visible. Like the electricity in lightning, or the wind of a hurricane, or wave energy in a tsunami, the effects of high-spirited karate training are obvious. It is accumulated and compounded in different forms of mental strengths and physical abilities. Its power can be harnessed, channeled, and unleashed by all of us with extraordinary results.

Sensei Stan Schmidt is an incredibly inspirational man to be around. His clinics are wonderfully packed with his stories of training in Japan. I first saw him in a Hollywood movie the 1980s with the legendary Masahiko Tanaka. We hosted some of his clinics in Central Illinois and I interviewed him for a couple magazine articles, but the most fun was often in the informal and spontaneous side conversations. He has charisma and charm. I asked him about the "karate spirit" and he told us several wonderful stories of his own experiences. This is one of my favorites:

He had been in a terrible car crash in South Africa, and both of his hips were crushed. Racked with broken bones and pain he was in the hospital and received two new hip implants. One night the pain was particularly unbearable, and he was moaning and complaining to his nurse. His body was broken and his spirits sorely diminishing. But his nurse teased and challenged him saying, "Aren't you one of those karate guys who are supposed to be tough?"

This hit home to a man that trained in Japan and with some of the toughest instructors and tournament champions in the world. So, he asked for a rock to be brought to his hospital bed. Every day he would use this flat rock for a portable makiwara. Schmidt said he that could not move his legs without excruciating pain for quite a while, but when he was in pain, depressed, and discouraged, he started to lightly tap on the rock with his knuckles. It lifted his karate fighting spirit to the forefront of his mind. Gradually, he said, the feeble taps raised his spirits and his taps gradually turned to punches until his spirits were lifted as his body slowly healed.

Another very real and obviously visible example is the *kiai*, or the "spirit shout." After all they are only sound and are technically invisible. But a proper "kiai," unleashed with the concentration of physiological and mental processes, is a very evident, explosive force to be reckoned with. It is well known as the high-decibel, startling yell that can literally terrify your opponent, cause pause in your attacker, and create a momentary hesitation in your bad guy. It assists you with coordinating and recruiting more muscle fibers into contraction. And, a *kiai* will time your breathing with your technique. Your blood-curdling scream and activity alerts and excites your own central nervous system into the equivalent of a self-imposed adrenalin injection. In the animal kingdom, predators roar and screech to momentarily stun or paralyze their intended dinner. Regardless of the outcome, your high-spirited energies and actions, demonstrate and explosive attitude, and animal-like commitment will be highly effective. Your spirit training will be very visible and stunningly real to your opponent. You are the stealth fighter: your spirit-training is your jet fuel and the wind under your wings.

Reflections

When I was a child walking along the bull grazing field on my grandfather's farm, I was often amazed at how harmless the tiny little single strand of wire looked that held thousand-pound Angus bulls at bay. Standing alone in the vast and peaceful field of wheat, I would double-dare myself to touch the wire, pinch it, and hold it for a count of one-thousand-one, one-thou… and ouch! That's about as far as I could get, when, from the harmless looking little wire, the invisible stream of electrons zapped my inquiring fingers, and I quickly felt the "spirit" of the wire, that very surprising extra zing!

A little wire is only a mild-mannered little wire until the extra invisible electron flow of energy is transferred through it; and then, *zing!* (On the other hand, I think I may have practiced my very first *kiai!*

"That which does not kill us, makes us stronger."

And so, it is with karate; to train only for the exercise, to gain some quick self-defense moves, or maybe just to win a couple of tournaments for plastic trophies, and take rank tests for new and pretty colored belts, are all rather superficial. Not that there aren't some benefits to be acquired: a slimmer waistline, cardio fitness, self-esteem, etc. Tournaments allow competition against unknown opponents. Rank tests encourage goal setting and practice. And even quickly learned self-defense moves may work on bad guys if you can remember them.

These are all good things. However, if you can tap into your own high-spiritedness and unleash your own normally hidden energies, then you can realize your true potentials. If we incorporate karate-do into our life style it can cause immeasurable changes for the best. You can experience skill levels you never dreamed of. To become the best karateka we can be, the best human being that we can be with combined physical and mental training.

Remember too that all efforts in karate-do transcend the dojo into other areas of everyday life that may be even more important to happiness and productivity. The more we can learn to tap into our hidden resources through martial arts, the more these new-found strengths can be used on demand. A *kiai* as energy, is a "button" to push to focus mental and physical resources on immediate challenges you must overcome. This is simply learning how to quickly rally skills and motivation together on command. These are learned skills. Let's say you have to change a flat tire and are turning bolts to remove the flat and all is going well until one lug nut stubbornly stops. You give it another try --- nothing! So you breath in, focus your mind and "Kiai!" to break it loose. This is an ordinary example of tapping into instant physical muscle-contracting energy beyond your normal output.

Let's look at another, more cerebral example where one would need to dig into both conscious and subconscious resources. Success is often said to be "when preparation meets opportunity." There are times that quietly drawing upon our best efforts on command can change our life and welfare! This is another high pressure, real-life situation. Let's say you have a job placement test or a final exam that your entire future depends on. The demand on you stressful but you must be calm, objective and mentally alert, digging deep for the correct answers. So, you prepare and study for the test (training), you enter calmly, but wide awake (good self-defense attributes), and in kind of "moving Zen," you go through the test allowing the best answers to surface.

In both cases, the mental or physical demands that could affect your immediate or long-range future and you are required to dig deep! Usually you will do best at what you practice the most. Karate-do is being prepared to react and conduct ourselves against all sorts of mental and physical challenges by tapping into our potential talent and strengths. We work toward training mind and body comprehensively and cohesively.

Now you can become the new source of your own fighting spirit. Martial arts training at higher levels causes new attitudes and paradigms, new energy levels, and new thoughts. All are channeled through you. You are the medium and the conduit for new and powerful constructive energies, never before realized.

Karate spirit training is beyond the norm. Karate is an art: you are both the medium. With maximum human potentials now waiting to be discovered, "Ready. Set. *Hajime!*"

Chapter 5

Correct Training
(Critical for Mind-Directed Movement)

THE CRITICAL IMPORTANCE OF TRAINING CORRECTLY is that the mind unconsciously directs the body to move in the manner we have trained to move. Correct training must be your daily priority and continuing goal; through persistence you may expect extraordinary outcomes. Karate is well known for its seemingly super-human power and movement. It is still fascinating to me as I write this, after five decades of karate training.

Correct training is critically important because you will get what you practice --- no more, no less. We train the mind and body to work together toward our intended outcomes. We do this in order to be able to unconsciously direct our techniques and movements at will, with minimal hesitation, and to maximize our human potential. Feverishly training incorrectly, resulting from a haphazard attitude, does not lead to our desired success. It only leads to wasted time, misguided energy, and results that are not dependable when we need them the most. Only attention to high quality training is the reliable path to the swift, mind-directed movement that may determine the outcome of life and death situations. We have untapped resources and extraordinary abilities to develop. This is no different than training for first responders or military for example. Correct leads to lifesaving successes, incorrect training does not. And when you are all alone under attack or in danger, you may not have time to dial 911. How you act without the luxury of time to think will depend on correct, repetitive, and intensive training.

Literally, your life may depend on it.

Unleash Your Free Spirit: "Direct" Intuitive Actions

According to Master Nakayama; "After a long period of practice, we can move unconsciously, freely, and properly."

Here's the thing: How well we move unconsciously is dependent on the quality of practice we have in our training. If we are undisciplined in the manner in which we practice, if we repeatedly do the wrong things at the wrong time and don't reflect and correct ourselves, or if we are taught incorrectly, then we react exactly as we train. If our life depends on our reaction time and taking the correct actions, we probably will lose. Like a computer, for example, if we put junk in, we will get junk out. If we train improperly, then we have trained our subconscious mind how to respond improperly. However, quality in equals quality out!

Researchers say that our subconscious mind does not filter what it takes in. It only takes the information that we give it at face value. If we train correctly this is all good, then we can "unconsciously" have appropriate skill sets and responses ready to go. But if we don't train correctly, frequently, and properly; sweating on the dojo floor, we may be in peril by our own lack of discipline.

Recent scientific research shows that we may surprisingly have eight layers of subconscious mind under our familiar conscious level. So, we have plenty of mental storage to use, and plenty of untapped power to draw from.

When attacked, with little or no time to think or to figure out a solution, our subconscious mind can react instinctively, just as Nakayama says above. After years of training to respond to thousands of attacks, one can respond instantly from the subconscious mind (freely), without having to think. If we have trained diligently, then we can respond intuitively and properly to the attack.

Basic Training and Real life

If you are a skeptic about the extreme value of the subconscious, think about this: Have you ever been driving to work, consciously solving the day's problems, or thinking about what you will do on the weekend? Then you snap to, and suddenly you don't recall the last few miles you've driven? You get that pang in your gut! You were on auto pilot?

Or do you recall putting shoes on before you left home today? Not so much: You've done it routinely your whole life and your subconscious easily directs your "putting-on-shoe technique." These are good habits formed.

When I was a child, I read that karate men were trained to react instantly to an attack without thinking; automatically. I was astounded! I vowed to learn this karate stuff. No matter what I had to do, I was going to learn this! I am not exaggerating. I was a child reading about this, and I was instantly hooked!

As far back as the 1600s, the monk, Takuan Soho, reportedly a mentor to and large influence on Miyamoto Musashi, the "sword saint of Japan," said that with proper training, "The function of the intellect disappears" (no time to think). "The arms, legs, and body remember what to do."

Now if you are an instructor and you want practical training methods to pass this along to your students there is really a rather simple formula that you can use. First, teach great quality basics. At first especially, don't overwhelm students with a wide variety, concentrate on strong repetitive fundamentals. They will have to do the same punching and kicking on their black belt test that you teach them in the beginning --- just a lot better of course!

The difference will be in the hundred thousand punches they have practiced in all sorts of situations over a long in-between. Techniques become internalized until they are done without thought. This can be applied to about any technique that you want your students to learn.

Hidetaka Nishiyama once told us in a black belt clinic at Shojiro Sugiyama's dojo in Chicago that most tournament champions continuously apply just one or two techniques that they score with instinctively and consistently with many opponents. This was a light bulb moment for me!

Along those same lines, we hosted Hirokazu Kanazawa, who told us that training in all karate techniques was necessary for us as students of karate. But for application for self-defense, fighting, kumite, etc., if a technique can be used in a hundred different situations it was valuable and dependable for survival. But if one technique could only be applied in one or two situations, then in was not at all a big priority for fighting. He said this was just something to keep in mind in daily training. This helps us establish training priorities.

I've told students that it's similar to other familiar activities like basketball for example. Michael Jordan didn't learn to fly with his extreme hang time to cram a basketball into the net without doing millions of baskets. Stephen Curry didn't learn to shoot 3 point shots without practicing millions of shots either. Even those phenomenal basketball players had to practice their basics correctly, and over and over with fierce determination. They made it look easy by extreme preparation until it becomes second nature.

If you are a beginning karate student or an intermediate student climbing through the ranks, and the black belts don't allow you to get in on them in sparring, and you are in awe at their fluid, seemingly effortless kata, do not be discouraged. That will be you after more and more repetition, practicing and training, and more time to let skill sets develop. You will slowly grow into someone who can move freely with your karate like has become part of you.

Remember, that in stressful everyday situations or when you are in a surprise attack faced with an imminent threat, you may have little or no time for thoughtful deliberation; your subconscious must bypass conscious thinking. It directs your body to move instantly and appropriately as if "the arms, legs and body remember what to do." This could literally save your life. There is no mystical secret here, just practice, practice, and more practice!

Chapter 6

Intuitive Action

ACCORDING TO MASTER HIDETAKA NISHIYAMA, assessing the threat and reacting to neutralize it must be done instantly and "are performed as a single momentary act."

He also said that "mind-directed reflexes don't have to think what to do." Historically, all of the great martial arts masters understood the absolute necessity of training to the point of subconscious, mind-directed action. This is the "pure action" of a highly trained individual.

Conscious thinking about what to do is unnecessary. This eliminates wasted time and reduces reaction time. Furthermore, seeing, perceiving, and reacting correctly to the threat are done instantly. According to Randall G. Hassell, "We practice until our techniques become second nature."

"Second nature" is quite simply to practice until our correct responses are as natural as a habit, done without the need to think. According to Hassell, we train and train and train until we reach a state of mind called "*myo*... the creative and original force emanating from the unconscious, from the original mind." This is like a "spider spinning its web."

The spider doesn't think about how or why it spins its web; it just does.

Myo is a perfectly natural state of mind, whereby the unconscious mind quickly and very naturally creates a solution to react appropriately to even the most life-threatening danger.

These masters, and many, many others through martial art history, reaffirm the importance of correct, repetitive training to elicit correct, unconscious responses to danger. We train until we bypass conscious layers of our mind and the top layer of thought patterns. We can unleash subconscious, free, spirit-directed techniques with tremendous power (as practiced correctly) in order to vanquish our attackers.

This is all an important facet of spirit training. As you may have guessed by now, to train the spirit, there is much, much more than meets the eye.

Reflections

Reflection and internalization of karate training is critical on many levels. Think and apply all you learn as you see fit, and don't be afraid to ask your sempai (your seniors) and your sensei for their interpretations. I often teach just one major concept at a time, and repeat teaching it in several different ways. Learning is best done in layers that overlap and support each other, that build upon each other. As the layers of knowledge and experience are stacked and fused tightly together like a Damascus sword blade, they provide much to draw from. Knowledge and skill sets become internalized layer upon layer, glued together by your karate spirit. The sum total becomes what you are, not just something that you do.

More food for thought: After a hard workout, step back and think about what you did, what you need to accomplish, and how to reach those goals. This reflection process sorts and frames thoughts into more meaningful patterns, and allows them to be absorbed. In your quiet moments, contemplate, reflect and absorb. You can then learn karate at the cellular level, into the depths of your subconscious. Internalize.

You can perform at your best on auto-pilot, triggered and guided by your intuition, with your technique flowing correctly and naturally: Living in the "now," doing what needs to be done millisecond by millisecond.

Chapter 7

Focused Mental Strength

MANY PEOPLE CANNOT CONCENTRATE on doing just one thing without being affected by irrelevant distractions. Some become easily distracted by their cell phones while driving with disastrous results. Often, they bounce from one distraction to the other like ping-pong balls. In kumite they can be easily tricked. Day to day, if this is a habit, they frustrate themselves and accomplish little. It's no wonder the smallest things can derail their day.

If faced with sudden life-threatening danger, they will crumble. With a lack of required mental focus, self-control or a sense of direction, they will probably not be able to draw on badly needed physical skills even if they have them. They will likely they just cave in. Every karate class incorporates mental focusing skills in nearly every activity. From making a proper fist, to blocking attacks, to performing kata, mental engagement is important every step of the way. We encourage students to continue applying those same skills outside the dojo to work, school and in all other phases of their lives. Most are quite surprised how well these new mental skills work. Adults understand quickly. So can kids, as soon as you tell them to use these new "powers" in taking a test in school and to not be distracted by friends and other things. We give academic awards to prove to them that building the mind is even more important than building the body. (Corresponding to the 5th of Gichin Funakoshi's *Twenty Precepts*.)

For students entering competitions or preparing for testing there are as many ways to improve mental focus as the instructor's imagination allows. In kumite you can have students spar with two students at once as they rotate into the "hot seat." For kata they can perform their kata with several students harassing them from all directions while they perform it. We've gone so far as to have one student perform their kata while the class bounces rubber balls off them from start to finish. The goal is to simply perform under abnormal harassment. Normal kata or sparring seems suddenly less stressful. These are merely a couple drills to teach a very serious mental concept. Since our students are trained to develop focused thinking in nearly every aspect of karate training, it is a point that is well driven home. Occasionally a drill as above can cause a "wow" moment of understanding.

In our quiet moments, it's important to reflect on what we need to do, and the different things we've learned and practiced in training. This can be valuable meditation. But some people just can't find a time and place to settle down to this Zen-like relaxation, therefore it becomes very beneficial as mental training is incorporated frequently into the normal karate class.

When bowing in and out of class formally, we sit in *seiza* (kneeling formally with both legs underneath), close our eyes and try do just that. The purpose is to calm ourselves, reflect on our training, and leave the day's goings on outside. We often recite the *"Dojo Kun"* or the "Dojo Code" in Japanese and English to remind ourselves of the principle-driven purposes in true karate. There is usually some discomfort --- especially at first --- that we must try hard to overcome. This teaches us and forces us to concentrate on our current training, while we refuse to be distracted by outside influences. After we all open our eyes, I sometimes joke with my students that karate kills germs, and that the pain will be all gone in a couple of years; my feeble attempt at karate comic relief. But then they laugh at the pain and get supercharged mentally for the challenges ahead.

Students quickly learn that as soon as they enter the dojo that we expect them to transform into karate-minded people; to leave daily events and troubles outside. I like to tell adults especially, that thinking only in terms of karate during this special class time is kind of like a little mini-vacation from all the baggage that they can leave outside as they bow in. As tough as the dojo training may seem, the challenges waiting outside are more real and fearful. Karate students appreciate meshing the skill sets of their karate training with the real-world experiences they need to face each day for the rest of their lives.

Our martial art literature is saturated with Samurai reflecting, meditating, letting thoughts sort and clear, even before a duel to the death. Here is a little practice mental exercise:

Imagine being outdoors on a warm spring day. Now imagine closing your eyes to feel the warmth of the sun on your face, a soft breeze flowing over you, smelling the fragrance of spring flowers and cherry blossoms floating gently to the ground. Imagine opening your eyes to gaze skyward to appreciate the joy of just being alive. Feel this picture gently settling on your mind. Visualize it as though it were real: feel the warmth of the sun, the gentle breeze; smell the fragrance. Think of this one experience and nothing else.

Try to understand the appreciation and zest for "living in the present" of the warrior. Nowadays for that matter, experience the same urgency of police, firefighters, soldiers, doctors, heart and cancer patients, or of any person who knows that death can be near; and yet they persevere. Much has historically been made about the samurai philosophy on the proper way to fight and die bravely. But the most important lesson to be learned is how to live bravely, live properly, live productively, and to appreciate each day. Cherish each moment. Take nothing for granted.

Chapter 8

Boldly Moving Forward

Keeping it Simple

IN MY LIFETIME OF TRAINING in traditional Shotokan karate, I have often been amused at the wide variety and colors of "stuff" that can be purchased and worn, for all sorts of activities and events. There is a rather tongue-in-cheek karate joke that paraphernalia marketing companies won't get rich from traditional karate students; all they feel they need is an occasional new uniform, a mouth guard and some hand guards. OK, maybe you'll see a club logo patch on a uniform or gym bag. But for the most part, the sequined, multicolored epaulets, spangled, satin-embroidered neon critters --- snakes, lions, scorpions, and such --- are, well, "the other guys."

A Simple Path to Extraordinary Growth

Entering the dojo for training in the martial way is not at all like merely stepping into a new exercise room. It is entering an entirely new way of thinking, clearly bringing about wonderful changes to lives.

There really can be no retreat if there is to be extraordinary personal growth. Progress is the realization of your new higher self-expectations. We must constantly try to raise our own bar.

In karate-do there must be only the unwavering search for improvement, for knowledge, ethics, health, fitness, truth and for conquering our weaknesses in meeting the challenges ahead, that life is guaranteed to throw upon us. According to Funakoshi, the mental strengths we accumulate through reinforcement of our karate principles are even more important than to be used in just self-defense and sport.

Once you enter the dojo, your life will never be the same.

Just think, if you only use karate to save your life just once, or save a loved one just one single time, then all your hard work has been well worth it. But there is much more. We need to build inner strength for the long haul. The karate life-style is a reservoir we can draw on for inner strength. Through serious training, our thought patterns change to a more positive outlook. We become much better prepared for adversity. In fact, we practice facing challenges that often seem impossible to overcome during each practice on purpose! Real life and death challenges can be incredibly humbling. They may come as complete surprises. Tragedies out of our control can suddenly attack us and our loved ones like accidents, illness, and the like. In seconds, lives can be changed forever. Even if we live a charmed life, as we age, our own bodies will turn against us! Seek to be strong and build up defenses because life is unforgiving for the weak and unsuspecting. Once you enter the dojo, change will be for the better, and you will never be the same. Train hard, move forward.

> *"If you are not moving forward, you are moving backward. Nothing stays the same."*
> -- GICHIN FUNAKOSHI

Reflections on Humble Beginnings

Back in 1968, I was sitting in my high school cafeteria with friends having a healthy diet of ice cream sandwiches and Coca Cola, while nervously chattering about our about our upcoming graduation. I noticed another senior passing out little white cards, and I overheard the word "karate" --- a very powerful magic word lurking quietly in the back of my own mind. I waved him over to take a card.

Reel back time to 1958, to me as an 8-year-old. When the bigger boys in our neighborhood were not beating me up, I was sitting in the grass most evenings, watching Bill McGath. Bill was a burly fireman who lived across the street from my house and who happened to be breaking boards with his bare hands. He was a very neighborly fireman who had been stationed in Japan for several years following World War II. I can only imagine who his instructors might have been. He studied karate and ju-jitsu, he told us, and very soon he had me doing basic blocks, punches, strikes, and throws in his front yard. The other kids would soon get bored and wander off. What were they thinking? I would stay and stay until my mother ordered me home. His grand finale was often an eye-popping board-breaking demonstration. We would beg and beg him to break something, anything! I was only 8-10 years old, but to this day I remember him breaking 2x4s against the grain. He showed me calluses on his brawny fire fighter hands, as I put my nose up to the boards for closer examination. He told me that he got that way from beating his hands over and over on hard wood, buckets of sand, rice, and stones in Japan. I was hooked! I spent my spare time slamming my tiny hands against bricks and boards to toughen them up like my karate hero. Hiding behind our garage and out of view of the watchful eye of my mother, I hammered away. My hands were bruised and raw, but I was determined to somehow change into a karate "expert." I desperately wanted the karate spirit!

I guess that would have been my first karate secret training, albeit primitive and misguided. Whack! Once, one of my kindling-sized boards actually broke (though probably from dry rot). It could just as easily have been my scrawny hand breaking, but I was lucky and very determined. Nevertheless, my spirit was launched; it soared. Of course my mother wanted to know why my hands were bruised. "I've been practicing my karate, Mom, like Bill across the street showed me."

The neighborhood "big dawgs" were not impressed with the scrawny neighbor kid's new hobby. So by day, I had to be a diplomat to avoid their beatings. And then I would faithfully return to my karate training and to any new secrets that I could pester my neighbor for. Occasionally, the beatings from the big guys sadly continued. One evening Sensei Bill showed me a nifty little technique he called *nukite* --- spear-hand thrust.

"Aim the points of your spear-hand attack right here," he said, pointing to his solar plexus. Now this seemed very interesting; he said it worked well against the bigger guys for a little guy like me.

A few days later, one of my larger tougher tormentors (and his sister, no less) verbally blasted me while I was strolling along minding my own business. The bully surged forward toward me, with his cheerleader sister in tow, telling what he was about to do to me to make his day (and ruin mine). I guess I had enough, and after all, my empty-hand arsenal contained a new spear-hand thrust. When he lunged at me, I drove my empty-handed spear into his exposed midsection with all my might. He immediately stopped in his tracks, doubled over, made heaving sounds and started crying. His sister started yelling at me for picking on her brother. Really? He never bullied me again. Never. Such was my introduction to karate technique application, compliments of my friendly fireman instructor who had trained in Japan.

Zoom forward ten years to high school. I took that card for free introductory karate lessons and drove to the dojo that very day. My karate embers had been warm and glowing; soon to become a blazing fire. I parked and walked up to the front screened door. I reached out for the door knob and froze. Someone inside yelled! I jumped. "Ichi! Ni! San! Shi!" someone bellowed from within.

"What the heck was that?" I thought. "Do I really want to go in there?" I took a deep breath, opened the door, and entered the dojo bravely. My life journey changed forever. I would never be the same.

Humility: A Supreme Karate Spirit

In the literature, karate training often was conducted in the yard of the sensei, often in the dark, often in secret, always in fierce determination, and always in humility. Where the training was, is of little importance. In karate all that is really needed is an instructor and a student, training and learning, and in the correct mindset. Training in karate is a lifetime goal; it becomes who you are. Karate is the art and you are the medium.

What Degree Are You?

One day after class, a wide-eyed parent emerged from the crowd of spectators to pick up his son. He pointed at my belt and said, "Is that a black belt?" It was a worn-out and ragged looking belt, more white than black, threads hanging in disarray, the once golden embroidered kanji barely recognizable.

A little embarrassed, I replied, "Yes Sir."

Seemingly amazed he prodded loudly, "Well, just what degree are you?"

I looked down at my tattered, shredded belt, shrugged my shoulders, grinned and said, "Just old, I guess."

Chapter 9

James Yabe: Humble "Offices?"

MY OFFICE IS MY GYM BAG. I carry everything from my clothing, uniforms and hand guards for sale, student handouts (a year's worth), awards to pass out, mouth guards, rank belts, first aid kits; well, you get the picture. My gym bag is my luxury karate office.

For that matter, in decades of teaching and training, my changing rooms have not been plush. I cannot count the number of restrooms and closets I have changed in. I was always pleased if there were no water puddles on the floor! But we often joked that, those puddles were the real reason for stances like *kiba-dachi*, horse stance, or straddle-legged stance. One of my longest karate students and friends, Ted Quinn, often tells of his surprise training in Japan, where at least at one tournament, everyone just climbed up into the bleacher seats, dropped their gym bags, and changed clothes all together, just standing around chatting in the bleachers. Most karateka are happy campers, but I'm not sure tournament organizers would get away with those changing room arrangements in the U.S. Most of the time, however, all we really need to train is a decent floor and a uniform and not always both of those at the same time.

I was joking about my portable karate office, my gym bag, with the very famous Sensei James Yabe. It was after one of Sensei Randall Hassell's ASKA clinics and Yabe Sensei was our prestigious guest instructor.

I had read about Yabe's exploits since the 1970s, in all the karate magazines of the time. I was so very happy that he was our ASKA Technical Chairman and Dan Examiner when I was promoted to 6th Dan. The only disturbing thought I had was that he looked to me to be 10 years younger than he was, and his technique resembled that of a 30-year-old! So, naturally, I wanted his autograph (just like any of the kids) and I was fumbling through my gym bag for something for him to sign.

All the while we were surrounded by fifty other anxious students who wanted to talk to him as well. I felt I was holding up the entire show and was certain I felt their eyes shooting lasers through my skull. Not to be discouraged, I kept fumbling, digging, and apologizing, while Sensei Yabe stood patiently smiling and waiting. I was a little rattled and frustrated by my disorganized state as I dived through my spare assortment of tape, bandages, and such, feeling like a big dork. I apologized to the karateka behind me again and again for holding up progress.

"This is usually my portable office that also doubles for my gym bag," I said.

Then surprisingly Sensei Yabe smiled and laughed. "Me too!" he said. "I always carry things back and forth stuffed in my gym bag, from work to practice after practice! Very confusing!" We had a good chuckle about our humble "offices."

CHAPTER 10

Funakoshi's Early Dojos
(And Other Beginnings)

FROM HUMILITY COMES THE EXPRESSION of the martial art in its purest, most beautiful, and powerful state. I often think of Funakoshi slipping through the trails, cloaked in the jungle darkness with his tiny lantern to train in his Master's back yard. And then, since he was a proper school teacher, he'd sneak back home before dawn. (Only sometimes a neighbor might see him.) Scandalous! Oh, my goodness! A school teacher rumored to be out all-night carousing about; scurrying around in the darkness with a tiny lantern. Just think of the results of his humble and sincere efforts to learn karate then. And now, just look around, surf the web! Millions of us worldwide do traditional Karate, thanks to the humble efforts and giant spirits of karate's founders.

Bare Bones: Setting the Compass

My first karate "lessons" were at age ten, on the front lawn of my Fireman-Sensei. These unquestionably set my compass toward karate training in the right direction for the rest of my life. In my own no-frills setting, my personal journey was launched; and while I couldn't know it at the time, my life and the lives of hundreds of my future students were influenced from that point on. A die was cast. No formal dojo, no floor, and no gi. Just a sensei and his rag-tag students, sitting on the ground: Karate instruction in its most basic form, simple but inspiring.

Karate-do: Raising Our Own Bar

We put on our Gi. Raise our own bar.
Raise our own standards. Heighten self-expectations.
We raise our achievement. We try to become a little
better each day… This is our karate spirit.

--- AUTHOR

Chapter 11

What is the Meaning of the "Art of Karate?

In the Words of Hidetaka Nishiyama

IN THE VERY EARLY DAYS OF MY TRAINING, Hidetaka Nishiyama told us that karate is a martial art that requires the practice, the development of basic skills, and the refinement toward perfection, just like other fine art forms such as extraordinarily beautiful music.

He said that if, for example, you take a musical instrument like a violin, that you have no clue how to play and give it a brave attempt, you will likely fumble around making disorganized noise; probably very annoying to even you.

But, if an expert takes it from your hand and plays a tune for you, you will instantly become fascinated with and appreciative of the very amazing contrasting results. You can watch and listen in awe!

Now if you go to a symphony combining 30-40 expert musicians with skills with multiple different instruments, all coordinated by a superb conductor with one single final goal in mind, you get beautiful, exciting, and inspirational results. It seems miraculous. The sum of physical and mental energy applied for a coordinated explosion of musical force is truly a breathtaking experience. This is all the result of disciplined training and practice.

Then, Nishiyama Sensei held one finger up at about his own head height and said, "This is the expert level of any beautiful art; music, painting, and the like."

Then, with the other arm, finger-extended and pointing downward, he made a slow upward sweeping motion until his lower finger touched his highest finger.

"Like all other art, we start from the beginning down here, where we can't do much, and practice until we get up to the expert levels of the art up here (at the peak). "It is this way with karate, too," he said.

That image was very sharp, fixed in my mind, and made the karate journey so clear. Like a beginning musician fumbling with tools of the trade to make screeching noises at first, we stumble around learning stances and twisting fingers and feet. But gradually, over patient practice and the passage of time we work toward the ever rising pinnacle of karate skill. And like any artist, we never reach "perfection" but the most important thing is that we stubbornly try. We keep going in the right direction and are enriched by all that we learn along the way.

Chapter 12

Karate's Man Behind the Message
Sensei Randall G. Hassell

THERE ARE THOSE WHO SAY that karate is simply another form of exercise or sport, and just what you see: punching, kicking, blocking, etc. They might contend that the extraordinary mental abilities, polished tactics and strategies, power-producing karate technique, and all, are just ordinary physical motions. Skeptics might say that the strong expressions of fighting spirit with karate sills are silly, unnecessary, and perhaps even useless; that they are a smoke-and-mirror karate myth.

Well, on the contrary, the results of high-spirited disciplined karate training are quite concrete, and easily seen for the trained eye. And this is vividly demonstrated especially if you are training with someone and are on the receiving end! When applied and practiced with serious, in-depth study, these principles allow you to attain much higher skill levels and a deep subconscious internalization.

Nakayama said that "At the highest stage, karate is applied without thought, from the subconscious levels of the brain." This is, of course, only after years of dedicated practice.

Fortunately for many of us, the application of these training principles can be learned for ourselves with our own serious study. Adaptations for age and physical ability can be made by varying activities and noting differences in strong points of student characteristics. The more experience an instructor has to draw from, the more effective the outcomes, working with differing student strengths and weaknesses. The rest usually depends on the student's desire and motivation for self-improvement. If they are willing to practice and practice, repetition after repetition, eventually they will triumph! Skill sets will become fluid, more natural, and can be done without forethought and hesitation.

Sensei Hassell often said that this "is like a spider and its web." The spider doesn't think about the beautiful geometric structure, the trees and buildings it hooks up to, or the length and width of its web. It just makes it because that is what it does. It is a spider. It makes its web to catch food because that's what it does to survive. Its behavior is innate. The web is synonymous with the spider. The spider is synonymous with its web.

Before you get the web in your face so that you can wildly swing your arms and sputter swear words at the spider, step back and look at the beauty in the shapes it has spun; and all just to live in its own way. The spider's martial art is its web. The spider doesn't think about it. It just does. And that is how we should train in karate: deliberate, dedicated, daily, just for the sake of training, like the spider and its web.

Similarly, just as the spider and its web are inseparable, so were Sensei Randall Hassell and his karate-do. I became aware of Randall Hassell's work and his ideals in the 1970s, from his regular column in BLACK BELT MAGAZINE. I had taught karate in the Illinois State University club and at the Central Illinois Karate Association while going to college to be an educator, and before serving in the military.

After the U.S. Navy, I started my new high school teaching job at Pekin Community High School. Just as soon as I could (in case I wasn't busy enough), I launched my own high school Karate Club on campus. I had some years teaching karate college age and adult classes, but high school students had special concerns that were new to me. These kids were as enthusiastic as ever, but they all had adolescent hormones and innate liabilities that were, well, a unique "characteristics" for me. Regardless, with my brand new secondary school teaching certificate, and my reasonably new black belt on my waist, I felt reasonably confident. Banzai!

Lucky for them, I was an idealist, and in addition to technique, I balanced my lessons with karate fire and brimstone, practically waiving Funakoshi's *Dojo Kun* and *20 Precepts* in hand. I had to reassure my principal and the school board that karate was good for citizenship and positive character building; that it wasn't the Hollywood movie violence of popular culture. This was never too difficult for me because I felt that I understood the general nature of traditional karate the way Funakoshi had intended: powerful technique with even more powerful emphasis on character building. This seemed to fit right into my new career setting.

In a timely fashion, Randall G Hassell's regular column, "The Karate Spirit," appeared in BLACK BELT MAGAZINE. It validated my weekly soapbox speeches. "Great!" I thought, "There is someone out there who's got it right! This guy thinks like me!" So, in addition to the rest of my resources, I was armed with the words of this JKA instructor that I had never seen. In fact, I would not meet Sensei Hassell for another ten years or so. Amazingly, many of my original karate club students that I taught far back then, are currently excellent black belts who teach and train, and are senior instructors in our Central Illinois Shotokan Karate Association and around the country.

Randall G. Hassell had written over a hundred articles, and written, co-authored, edited, and published over 25 books on Shotokan Karate. He wrote about all manner and aspects of karate techniques, kata, karate philosophy, history and biographies. He has written about the legends --- Masatoshi Nakayama, Osamu Ozawa, Hidetaka Nishiyama, Stan Schmidt, James Yabe and Edmond Otis, to name a few. He had even helped upstarts like me, Carl Hartter, and James Hartman with our own articles and DVDs, like the *Shotokan Masters Series*.

Since his first class with Hidetaka Nishiyama when he was twelve years old, Hassell dedicated the rest of his life to contributing to Shotokan karate and its students. At his passing, Sensei Randall Hassell was both the Chief Instructor of the American Shotokan Karate Alliance (ASKA) and the President of the American JKA Karate Association (AJKA). As Karate's Great Communicator, he gave inspiration and enthusiasm, spreading karate-do from coast to coast.

This is the spirit of tempering the purely physical wild-eyed violent potentials of a martial art with the purposeful, thoughtful, and character-building calmness that is at its heart. Sensei Hassell set a high benchmark, just as the karate he taught. Why? Why does the spider spin its web?

Chapter 13

Karate Empowering

You and your training are inseparable

Does the man move the sword, or does the sword move the man?

WE SHOULD TRAIN AND INCORPORATE KARATE into our everyday lifestyle to experience the maximum benefits. After years of training, in fact, technique eventually seems as comfortable and normal as an old pair of favorite tennis shoes. It seems like it just becomes part of us. This is so very important because techniques become far easier to use and they are with us all the time if we need them. We train until karate is merely an expression of who we are and not just something that we do. It benefits us most like the original intent of the great masters if it is assimilated into our behaviors, attitudes, and actions.

This is an important reason for only practicing "correct" karate training. Simply put, if we practice something incorrectly and erratically, it's not going to be a great reflexive life-saving skill we can depend on. If life or death can be decided in our instant success or failure, in choice or application, of a skill we could have worked a little harder to improve, then the effort and quality of practice we invest becomes quite critical. It's not always about saving ourselves. More important can be the responsibility we have for the safety of our children, spouse and other loved ones. Well-rounded, consistent karate consciousness becomes even more effective than electronic security measures.

Every bad habit that we would love to leave behind is one that we've practiced, maybe unknowingly, until we can't shake it off! I hate it when that happens. So, if we understand that practicing good habits from basic through advanced training means that we are internalizing good karate habits and skills, that knowledge is a powerful tool. When karate is as natural as breathing, and can be applied suddenly with correct intuitive actions, you become a very highly skilled and dangerous person. You can apply explosive, mental and physical energy (fighting spirit) through the conduit of your body in the form of well-honed technique. At that instant, the idealistic and invisible suddenly becomes highly visible, highly focused, and an unusually effective survival skill. Train the body. Train the mind. Electrify your energy!

We often speak of "fighting spirit" as being intangible, but the results of its strong presence are outstanding, impressive and vivid. Energy is applied to change the clenched fist that anyone can make, into a powerful weapon with destructive power. Fighting spirit is an animating life-force.

Of course, technical skills can be memorized and practiced, and seem very impressive to the untrained eye. But it is when the mind and body are trained and fused together as one that karate flows according to the instantly changing demands of the situation.

Empowering

Karate uniquely fulfills universal needs for unarmed human survival and development. Unfortunately, some people come into karate class with a feeling of lethargy, seemingly beaten down by life's challenges. They may have been bullied by unknown "others," by aggressive family members or schoolmates, have experienced tragedies or illness, or other overpowering circumstances causing them low self-esteem and the like. Everyone has their own burdens. If they can buy into long-term karate training, their spirit, their self-esteem, their confidence, enthusiasm, and motivation will all increase. Negative feelings cannot be switched on and off. They take time and positive influences to turn around. An important part of the life-changing positive potentials in modern martial art schools is not just the training, but also in being surrounded by other positive minded people who may have come through similar trials and tribulations. Students gradually become empowered and strengthened, mentally and physically. In the dojo, they are surrounded by high-spirited, like-minded people who are all working toward higher ideals. Success breeds success. They will become newly empowered to take initiatives, and to be proactive in their own life. One of the most spectacular qualities of karate-do is that it strengthens while exploring untapped power and potential to assist in realizing all sorts of goals and dreams. Some may think these claims over reach, but instructors who have been working with students for a while or are well traveled all have their own success stories to tell.

In addition to community dojo experiences and benefits, as students attend other clinics and tournaments, they make new friends, share experiences, and soon realize that they are not alone in their challenges and that they are in good company with others in the same boat.

Barriers to Speed Bumps

Studying the works of many of the great masters you may have noticed common traits. They all seem to have a strong sense of clear vision with an equally matched determination, to cause materialization of that vision. This is no different than many people who excel in any field. In karate we teach people to develop short term visions or goals, to work toward and accomplish them, and to use that accomplishment as a platform to work toward the next goal. By its very nature in day-to-day training, karate students get the courage to establish a goal and they acquire the confidence and ability to believe in themselves. If they can believe in themselves and channel their energies, then they can learn to turn vision into reality. If they can keep going and are not easily discouraged, eventually they can succeed. If they can visualize themselves realizing dreams, they can learn to make them reality. As instructors, we are "success coaches" and through karate-do, students can apply their success-building skills to all other challenging events and issues in their lives. Karate students can learn to see barriers as mere speed bumps.

Chapter 14

Transcendence and Bringing People Together

Transcending Barriers

THE POWER OF COMMITMENT defies measurement and is a driving force in *Budo*. Life cannot be the same for those who enter the dojo and welcome the challenges and rigors of karate-do. Karate is the art, mankind the medium. Just as crude scrap metal can be forged into beauty by the stern and discipline eye of the sculpture, so can the human spirit be changed in karate-do. This means an uncompromising search for improvement, for knowledge and for ethics to conquer weaknesses and accept challenges.

This is the story of one ordinary man's persistence to achieve his vision. Karate kinships have the power to transcend different cultures, races, religions, politics, nationalities, and lands that are oceans apart.

Ted Quinn was in my first high school Karate Class and absorbed all instruction like a sponge. When we first met, Quinn was a scrawny teenager; awkward, shy, and very polite. As I twisted his fingers into his first satisfactory fist, I couldn't have known he would later fight as the only American member on an elite Japanese military karate team in the All Japan Karate Championships in the Budokan.

As I quoted Master Nakayama in class, I would never had thought my student would be training in Master Nakayama's memorial workout that was held in the Hoitsugan dojo where Nakayama lived and taught. And during our high school clubs first big demonstration, Quinn made a 180-degree wrong turn in a group kata. Feeling his pain and being sympathetic, I could not have envisioned him near the Imperial Palace years later, receiving an Outstanding Kata Award from the Minister of Defense of Japan.

By the end of his first 6-year stint in Japan, he was the lead Instructor of the Yokota Air Base Karate Club, spoke fluent Japanese, and was a member of the Japan Karate Association's (JKA) Ebisu military team.

So, how does a *gaijin* from the Corn Belt of Illinois end up in an elite Japanese team in the All Japan Karate Championships? Ted Quinn was in my first high school Karate Club class and absorbed instruction like a sponge. He was my first student to attain the rank of shodan. He loved all things karate. After receiving Nidan, he joined the USAF and was stationed in Japan, finally realizing his dream.

He first trained with Aoki Sensei, a 5th Dan in Shotokan Karate International (SKI) who taught Quinn *kata Unsu*. When Aoki Sensei told Quinn, he was going to teach him Unsu for him to perform in competitions, Quinn said he thought, "No way!" But Aoki took Quinn under his wing and it went well.

Quinn taught at the Yokota AB during the week when he decided to enter the All Japan Self-Defense Force Championships, where he competed with hundreds of black belts. He made many Japanese friends including Yoshitoma-San, a four-time Japan Self-Defense Force kumite champion, who invited him to train at the headquarters branch of the JKA in the Hoitsugan dojo. In addition to his Air Force and Yokota karate classes, he took the train weekly to train with the Japanese military team at Ebisu. At Ebisu, he said, workouts were always four hours long and always basics --- sparring, Heian and black belt kata. He was thrilled to train although if he received a bloodied injury during practice, he said he would get some weird looks on the train ride back home.

By surprise, just a week before the JKA All-Japan Championships, he was invited to compete *with* the Japan Self-Defense Force Team. My Central Illinois home-town karate student was in heaven on earth --- more that living his karate dream in Japan.

Although his Ebisu military team fell short of the finals, two competitors won all of their *kumite* matches. One was Yoshitoma Sensei, the four-time champion, the other person was my *gaijin* student, Ted Quinn.

He fought in the Budokan and in local tournaments for the rest of that first six years. His Japanese team earned fourth place in one All Japan Championships, and Quinn won several local tournaments. He showed his Japanese friends our black belt test videos back in Illinois and they were very pleasantly surprised that in our US, Central States Shotokan karate gave so many Japanese commands! Quinn says after his initial training with us back home, he had no trouble transitioning to training in Japan. Good karate is just good karate everywhere.

Quinn was an NCO (Non-Commissioned Officer) in Intelligence Information and many of the Japanese Karate instructors he trained with were commissioned officers in the

Japanese Defense Forces. He was pleasantly taken off guard and quite honored at some USAB functions that were mixers involving both Japanese and U.S. commissioned officers that he had to attend. Out of nowhere, he said, Japanese officer karate instructors would bypass their U.S. counterparts and trot over to cheerfully shake hands with him and start talking about karate training, leaving Quinn's superiors scratching their heads.

After his Tokyo/Yokota AB years, he spent another six years in Northern Japan on the Misawa AB. There he taught classes to Japanese students, especially youth classes. Unlike some American parents it seems, Japanese parents would frequently tell him to yell at and get tough with their children if they were "less than enthusiastic." Quinn, does admit that kids are kids and often have the same "growing pains" in any country. He speaks and writes Japanese fluently. He was always amused at the deer-in-headlights expressions when he started shouting and ordering them around in their native Japanese as he taught. He was the subject of Japanese newspapers and TV interviews as a goodwill ambassador between Americans and Japanese, and he was praised by his military officers for the same.

Quinn made many lifelong Japanese friends during his twelve years there. With the spirit of Karate-do as the common bond, he built wonderful relationships, literally overcoming oceans bringing our cultures together; people to people.

He is just one example of the ambassadorship qualities of karate-do that transcend barriers of nationalism, race, religion and politics, because karate fulfills the universal needs of human development and survival that bonds people together.

CHAPTER 15

The Spirit of Worldwide Harmony
Hirokazu Kanazawa

HIROKAZU KANAZAWA TOLD US that, "Funakoshi Sensei often said that harmony among people is one of the most important qualities of karate." As we look back, we were so very fortunate to have one of the original Shotokan legends all to ourselves for several days in the late 1980s. When he wasn't teaching our clinics, we picked his brain over anything we could think of, from his hallmark kicking skills shown in the *Best Karate* series, by Nakayama, to his future with SKI, or his memories of training under Gichin Funakoshi. Kanazawa was always animated with our students, young and old. He took particular joy, it seemed, to let the kids kick his hands, as he held them higher and higher for them to reach.

The rewards of karate-do are great as you will know from your own feelings of self-improvement. Very often, those benefits are transferred from person to person, instructor to student, friend to friend, and so on. In other words, they are shared from one human being to another.

Carl Hartter and I stood waiting at the Bloomington airport watching for our hero's plane to land, pacing back and forth with anxious anticipation. With great pride, my brand-new luxury Chevy van would be our "limo" to usher Sensei Kanazawa around. We were extremely excited about meeting Sensei Kanazawa, who had already been a legend for decades. We each had our own collections stacked of his books, ready to ask him to autograph with his signature Mt. Fugi flare!

Unfortunately for my male ego, before heading to the airport, as I picked Carl up at his house, I promptly backed into and demolished his mail box. It caved in the back door of my week-old van. The long glimmering chrome ladder was mangled like a pretzel and the door sharply creased into a nice 3-foot "V." I sheepishly half-heartedly attempted to straighten his mail box to an upright stance. I knew that my very good friend would never let me forget this any time soon. We immediately headed for the airport to get Kanazawa; a perfect start to an already exciting day.

As we greeted Sensei and helped with his luggage, his warmth, humility and charm were magnetic. We opened my shiny wrinkled door to load his luggage. Carl, true friend that he was, enjoyed explaining in lengthy detail how I had remodeled my new door just an hour earlier. Kanazawa Sensei's eyebrows raised, and his face lit up with a big smile.

"You did this?" he said, pointing and grinning from ear to ear. So much for me breaking the ice and establishing credibility as a serious, credible host with one of the most famous karate masters in the world. "Lucky" for me, it became the running joke for the rest of his trip. He had a terrible cold and probably a fever, but he was always cheerful, energetic, and clearly appreciative for even the smallest assistance or consideration given him. He held nothing back from his teaching.

At this time, Kanazawa Sensei was teaching in more than 60 countries including some not-so-friendly countries in the Middle East. Of course, Middle East tensions are always high. And things have changed a lot for the worse in that part of the world since then. But there are still good people everywhere. Over lunch with a big bowl of hot chicken soup, Sensei related stories of teaching in one Middle Eastern country, and then rather nervously traveling to neighboring countries to teach. Kanazawa said that all of the karate students, without exception, in all of the countries where he taught, were high-spirited, dedicated, and friendly karate students. He said that they all extremely excited to see him and treated him very, very well. Karate was the common thread among the students, even though their respective governments were political and military adversaries who were always at odds with each other. He jokingly admitted that he was very aware of, and at times quite startled by, the sheer number of machine-gun-carrying guards at all the airports.

"Everybody had guns," he said, "and they all looked mean!"

In our private and thoughtful conversations when we had him to ourselves, he repeated often that one of the "most important things that karate has to offer is harmony among all people." He was clearly an ambassador of good will in his travels.

As he taught our large mixed classes, composed of beginners to our crustier veteran black belts, and he gave special attention to the kids. He would chuckle while holding out his hand for them to kick. His warm friendliness was genuine. His sessions were enlightening, inspiring and challenging. He happily posed for pictures and signed autographs with his signature Mount Fuji for everyone. I presented him an oil painting of Mount Fuji that I had painted as a going away gift. He smiled and thanked me saying that he and his son had climbed it together. He was the perfect guest instructor and lived up to every bit of his legendary leadership reputation.

The trip was yet to be more challenging for me, no matter how hard I tried to be a good host. When Carl and I picked Sensei up at the hotel to drive him to Chicago's O'Hare Airport, I hurried to pick up his beautiful zebra-skinned gym bag that students in Africa had given him, when suddenly, to my embarrassment (and horror), both handles ripped off into my hand. There I was, literally standing in his room with the two torn handles in my hand; the bag still resting defiantly at my feet. This was truly a rare moment. Hoping for a mythical knockout punch from him, to spare me shame, I just stared at the bright zebra bag on the floor, and then at the handles in my hand in disbelief. "Oops!"

"Oh, don't worry." he chuckled, "Its ok. It's old anyway." He casually pulled another brand-new gym bag from a selection in his suitcase, and off we went!

On the way to Chicago's O'Hare Airport, Illinois farm terrain is flatland as far as the eye can see. Kanazawa Sensei was clearly exhausted and recovering from his bout of flu. And yet, he expressed continued surprise at our flat landscape. He would look astonished that he could not see a mountain. He politely asked if he could take a nap. (I'm going to say no?) He took his shoes off, stretched out, and dropped off for a well-deserved nap. He would sleep a while, wake up, look back and forth out the windows, and again, puzzled, ask, "No mountains?"

"No mountains, Sensei. Sorry," we said.

When Carl and I checked him in at the airport, the attendant looked at his passport with startled amazement, turning page after page, looking at the wide assortments of stamps. I smiled and said, "Mr. Kanazawa travels a lot."

Kanazawa Sensei traveled worldwide to teach. His work and dedication has touched millions of lives, bringing lessons of harmony; lessons of true karate-do. And as he said that his teacher, Gichin Funakoshi, had intended "to bring harmony with karate-do to people world-wide," Kanazawa said, "This is the most important thing about karate."

Chapter 16

Lessons from a Samurai
Osamu Ozawa

Meeting a Samurai

THE WORD *SAMURAI* MEANS "to serve," and Osamu Ozawa certainly conformed to that definition. Since he started training in karate-do, he served the karate world well.

In one sincere, quiet moment, Ozawa Sensei looked me directly in the eyes and said, "Every time I put on my uniform I am ready to die." Then he raised both eyebrows and said, "You understand?"

"*Oss!*" I replied. It seemed simple enough, especially considering the source; I understood immediately. He was a direct student of Master Gichin Funakoshi, and at that time he was, in fact, the most senior Japanese Shotokan instructor in the Western Hemisphere.

Ozawa Sensei was from a very traditional samurai-heritage family in Japan. Fortunately for us, Randall Hassell was a good friend of Sensei Ozawa and happened to be writing Ozawa's autobiography called, *A Samurai Journey*. This afforded many of us wonderful training opportunities and some very animated candid conversations from him. I, for one, was glued to every word.

Ozawa told us that at the very end of WWII, he was a scared teenager, but responding to his country's last desperate call, he became a *kamikaze* pilot, in the context of his family's historic samurai traditions.

Ironically, at exactly the same time, my own father was a young 17-year-old sailor in the United States Navy serving on ship in the pacific. He was an anti-aircraft machine gun operator on a troop carrier. Although he never had to engage an air attack, he always told me his main worries were *kamikazes* and submarines. In fact, one day a Japanese submarine surfaced next to his ship. My father and his friends were tremendously relieved to find out that they were surrendering. I am so very, VERY happy that my father and Ozawa Sensei's paths never crossed back then; small world!

One fateful day Ozawa's number came up to go on his final mission. His plane crashed on takeoff, flipping upside-down so that the bomb strapped under the plane's belly didn't explode. The crash left him in traction with multiple broken limbs, collapsed lungs, broken eardrums, and other assorted injuries. While he was still in traction in his hospital bed, Japan surrendered, and the war officially ended. He would finally be able to go home. Sadly, upon arriving at the vacant lot where his family had been, he found everything laid to waste, flattened by one of atomic bombs. All he said that he found was a piece of wood with a note about a possible location of his family might have gone. When he did locate his family, he said they were extremely astonished, to say the least, and elated to see him because they thought he was dead. Several weeks earlier they had conducted Sensei Ozawa's funeral. His life seemed pretty much at rock-bottom, but the fire in his samurai-spirit would not be diminished.

"Seven times down, eight times up!"

As you would see if you read his auto-biography, Ozawa would not stay down long. He would later become a TV director in Japan, even directing actors Clint Eastwood and Rita Moreno! He was extremely motivated and creative. He became a millionaire and a pauper several times. His high spiritedness always reminded me of the quote, "Seven times down, eight times up!"

We were able to host Ozawa in Central Illinois several times and we took teams to his Las Vegas tournaments as well. We all enjoyed his clinics and long dinner visits in Central Illinois and in St. Louis as well. His classes were riveting, and his real-life stories were fascinating. There is one conversation I will never forget. Oddly enough, I saw Ozawa Sensei sitting roadside on the curb, in front of the dojo on a very busy street in St. Louis. I walked over and joined him. I found myself sitting side by side with Sensei on the curb with our feet alongside the road with heavy noisy traffic. He was animated and excited as we talked about training, and he reminisced about his early training experiences. I gave him my full attention, of course, but our feet were dangling out in the road and I thought we were going to be road kill (in the literal sense) any second!

He wanted to tell us why he started karate. He said that he started karate because he "was so very terrible at playing baseball!" He told us that his parents were not pleased about him "wasting time with that funny karate stuff." If that was so, I know many karate people who are happy that he wasn't a baseball star.

He told us how he, Nakayama Sensei, and other great instructors of their generation struggled to bring karate to the forefront of public recognition with credibility. This was post-World War II and at first karate was not always welcomed by everyone in Japan. Ozawa Sensei showed us the scars on his forearms from sword attacks to prove this point. But all these great men were convinced, just as Funakoshi had taught them, that karate was a powerful force for ethical human improvement worldwide. Ozawa stressed to all that one of the most important aspects about "this beautiful martial art" was bringing people together on common ground. No matter "who you are or where you come from", he said, "Because we all sweat together out on the dojo floor, working on the same goals, we can become friends."

Since I was very young, I always enjoyed listening to the reflections of my elders, to see things through their eyes and to learn from their life experience. Sensei Ozawa was an outstanding, memorable example. He was so eager to teach and share from his life, and his stories and perspectives were fascinating. Once when he visited our Central States dojos, the first Gulf War was on. In a free moment of down time and especially in the evenings after practice, he would join with Randall Hassell and Carl Hartter, and we would sit together to watch Desert Storm on CNN. He was fascinated by it. He told me that Sadam Hussein had made a huge miscalculation of America's spirit and technology. He told us that Japan had underestimated America's technology and tenacity as well, in WWII. As we sat and watched with him in his hotel room one evening, Ozawa Sensei "cheered on" American forces in the Gulf War as he watched and we joined him in a cool beverage.

A Lesson in Courtesy

Osamu Ozawa was a perfectly charming gentleman, but make no mistake, karate with his upbringing was the fire in his belly, and he was truly from samurai stock. Ozawa was one of those people that, when he entered a room, all eyes were on him. His mere presence would attract everyone's attention. But as captivating and genuinely friendly as he was, he was the real deal: one of Funakoshi's direct students.

Randall Hassell, Carl Hartter and I ushered Ozawa Sensei into the crowded college gym for morning clinic. As we walked through, the early morning group seemed sleepy, some sitting on the floor talking, some quietly stretching, and so forth. We took sensei to the locker room to get ready for the day. As we walked back into the gym I yelled, "Line up!"

I bowed the class in, made opening remarks, and introduced Sensei Ozawa to the group. I bowed to Ozawa

Sensei and turned the class over to him. Surprisingly, he promptly started sternly chewing out the lined up class, especially higher ranks, for not taking the time to formally and courteously greet their own senseis. "You should have bowed and said, good morning, Sensei!" when we came in. "You should show your own sensei respect!" He was emphatic. But it wasn't about him at all. It was about the lack of proper etiquette our students had shown by not greeting us. Needless to say, our students were wide awake and VERY attentive to etiquette and all other aspects of training the rest of the weekend.

Osamu Ozawa was a good task-master. He could change from grave seriousness to cracking a joke in an instant. He would not just teach technique. He gave amazing and unique perspectives on karate's historic background, on the details of what Funakoshi stressed on making a punch, for example. He was so very happy to sign autographs, talk with the children, and pose for pictures with everyone after class. When he spoke, everyone listened! I treasure meeting him and the many hours of listening to his stories, his reflections and his advice. Ozawa seemed to me to be a very real and priceless link to the origins of authentic traditional karate.

Chapter 17

Spirit Training Essentials

THE FOLLOWING ARE ELEMENTS of spirit-training that are to stimulate thoughtful reflection. These are relatively short items with often poignant words, phrases or paragraphs. Taken separately or in combination, they can be read lightly, laid down and revisited. They are only meant to provoke thinking and require no agreement or disagreement. Depending on context or your point of reference, they may challenge or reinforce existing paradigms. They are here for your consideration as small components in mix of the bigger picture of *Karate Spirit Training*.

Do Not Be Shallow

Those who do not practice Karate seriously cannot understand. The true rewards of karate-do, of budo, the lifestyle of the karate student, are not relegated to a collection of colored belts, plastic trophies, ribbons and medals and other things.

This is superficial. This is shallow. Rewards are measured by training, conviction, maturity, growth, and friendships from countless hours of dedicated practice on the dojo floor.

Keep the "Beginner's Mind"

You can never know enough. Some people just put in time, doing karate for exercise, or for other superficial reasons like tournaments or belt tests. At some point they may think they know it all. They do not.

Be a beginner every day. Learn as if everything is new.

Learn from all things. Try to develop as much mental and physical skill as possible to sincerely become a better human being.

The All-Important Journey

Our karate journey is our goal. The longer we can maintain this journey, the better human being we become. Then, we have accomplished our true purpose in karate training. Winning the match, winning a trophy, passing the rank exam, getting a diploma or a brand new colored belt --- these are merely artifacts of resting points along the way.

They really have no lasting significance. Karate is designed to strengthen our weaknesses, letting us investigate ourselves more honestly. The experiences, the training, the adaptation of the body and mind, the changing attitudes and paradigm shifts, the shoring up of our spirit to break through new barriers, are what are important. The development of the human being is the never-ending goal.

Think of karate as steel guard rails on a treacherously winding mountain road. We must keep going forward under our own steam, but the "karate guard rail" keeps our journey on track.

Pain: Friend or Foe?

Pain is most disabling in the absence of purpose, exhilaration, determination or joy.

- By itself, pain does not have to have power over you.
- Accompanied by enthusiastic goals, it is diminished.
- Accompanied by obsession, it can become a friend.

Mountains Are Only Paradigms

A paradigm shift is a dramatic contrasting shift in perspective (often accompanied by a major "light bulb" moment). In karate, expect them often. They can cause us to see something in an entirely different light from what we had perceived before. In karate training, paradigm shifts in the process of personal growth are quite common, beneficial, and even required. They are accompanied by a change in the way something is understood to be. This is much more profound than merely changing your mind. It is a major change in point of view. It changes inner feelings.

Consider a mountain. To some, it is an extraordinary obstacle, something to go around, to avoid. They cower in its shadow. Their heart sinks with fear and inferiority as their eyes look skyward toward the peak. Impossible!

Others see the same mountain as a beautiful challenge—a friend to embrace in order to become stronger. The attitude and goals concerning the mountain, the paradigm of a martial artist, should be to embrace the journey with fresh enthusiasm. Embrace the challenges to overcome bravely and appreciate the lessons to be learned with the new strengths to be acquired.

Welcome the wind in your face. Breathe deeply the thin, clean air. Fight the incline until your legs feel like they are going to explode and rejoice at the profound visuals of each step upward to the summit where you will feel exuberant with satisfaction as you gaze over the carpet of landscapes below.

Two different points of view, same mountain.

Teaching and Learning:
No One Can Teach You Karate

This does not reflect on one's IQ. I have trained in karate for fifty years and I have a Master's Degree in Education with thirty-five years teaching experience in high school. I did not state that to boast; quite the contrary. I said it to help students understand that we cannot really "teach" them anything. They must learn it.

I can only really be an expert at making things understandable for students to help them learn. I can speak clearly, demonstrate vividly, and I can set up all sorts of karate individual or partner drills and learning experiences; they will learn by experiencing and doing.

Most people think that teaching is somehow a process to insert knowledge. I could, of course, punch you in the nose to illustrate the value of basic blocking. I would be hoping that this abrupt action will ensure you are encouraged and motivated to learn quickly to block, and I would gain your attention, and I would be fairly certain you would retain this "learning," but I cannot "insert" blocking abilities into you. I cannot force-feed learning. However, we can clearly offer strong incentives.

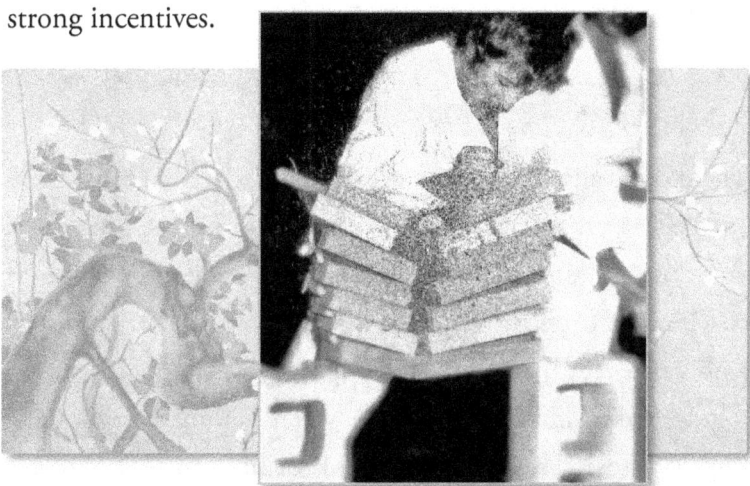

In fact, one of my first instructors apologized that he had no "black belt pill" to give us. The only way to learn is to be a sponge. Absorb all that you can. Relive learning experiences and practice them.

Instructors quickly understand what I mean when working with a child that the parent insists take karate against the child's will. This is not a rewarding situation for either the child or for the instructor. We might try to impress them with tornado-kicking-cartwheels, but unless they are motivated to learn, we will have little success teaching them anything.

Through experience, we gradually accumulate more and more teaching strategies and tactics to help larger numbers and varieties of student abilities.

Of course, this is something we really can't be taught, until by practice, trial and error, we learn to do it ourselves… No one can teach us. Guide our learning, yes.

Something to think about.

Make It Real!

The more realism a learning situation has, the better the lesson will be learned. A teacher can explain all day how to use a chain saw, but unless you grab that bad boy saw and get some coaching on operation and safety, you should have an ambulance nearby. We can explain how a rising block works, but it makes much more sense when a punch is zooming toward a nose! This is a basic law of teaching and learning.

This concept of preparing the mind and body for stressful situations is a universally valuable one. Here are some familiar examples:

If you are in combat or law enforcement training, you will be subjected to many very reality-based simulated scenarios where you might be shot at, and you have to respond flawlessly. If you are a medical practitioner, from doctors to nurses and support staff, you will be practicing accidents, illnesses and disaster emergencies using CPR, trauma care, types of first aid, and the like. If you become a teacher for any grade level, you will spend weeks in front of real students learning teaching methods, discipline, counseling and class management. If you are a rodeo clown, I highly recommend on-the-job training before you are the only colorful target in front of a raging bull. To teach a teenager enough driving skills to get that first driving license, most states require the youth to spend fifty or more hours driving with a very nervous parent. So, likewise, it stands to reason that the best way to learn how to fend off an attacker is to practice being attacked! Learn by doing.

Show a Strong Intent!

Osamu Ozawa stressed often:

"When you train with a partner in the dojo, you must always, when you are in the role of the attacker, show a visibly strong intent to hit them."

Even in a drill where our attack is purposely stopped short, our facial expression, high-spiritedness, body language, and *kiai*, all must convey the clear and dramatic "intention" to make a very real attack.

When partner training, convey a high-spirited intensity in attacks. This situation sets up learning experiences that are powerful. Students learn to face an opponent that has a strong aggressive spirit, while using the techniques being practiced. Partners learn to apply techniques under emotional pressure, much as will be required in self-defense. They learn to project a strong spirit in the face of aggression and danger. The more real the simulated situation seems, the more students can internalize skill sets they can really use under duress.

CHAPTER 18

Awareness
The Extraordinary, Aware and Prepared Spirit

Different Kinds of Awareness

ANY INSTRUCTOR WORTH A DIME teaches awareness to students from the beginning. Being aware of everything around you all the time is ideal, but its total mastery is not realistic, given our human frailties. However, it is an essential goal to shoot for. Being aware of all that is around you, or all that could be a potential risk or threat, is not foreign to a police officer answering a late night call, a firefighter entering a blazing inferno, or an infantry soldier stalking through a "hot zone." Remember that karate training is "life training" that helps us both in our day-to-day existence, and in those unusual, potentially high-risk situations. A calm, alert, or active, state of awareness is essential for someone walking alone, day or night. It is essential for driving home from work during rush hour. It is essential for a teacher responsible for the safety of hundreds of students.

My best training in the full meaning of awareness came early in my training. I guess karate training in the 1960s was often likened to the "school of hard knocks." My first instructor trained in Northern Japan. Classes for him in Japan ranged from harsh to brutal, and he seemed to be obligated to pass many of those methods along to Carl Hartter and me.

Maybe I wasn't great, but I was brave, and I refused to give up.

I was a Shodan after 4 years of college with a lot of tough training in kumite, self-defense, kihon and kata. In the military, we had Marine drill instructors who delighted in reinforcing my martial arts mental toughness. Awareness became even more challenging as a teacher in hallways surrounded by 500 students at a time as I observed them "all," with all my sensors dialed up to high!

I thought I had the "awareness thing" pretty well under control, until I decided to be a private aircraft pilot. Oops! My "light bulb moments" soon became neon. Suddenly, global awareness not only meant what was left-right-center-and behind, but also anything above and below and in all directions, every second; monitoring the instruments to insure you were not upside down, sideways, too fast, or too slow so that you don't crash and burn. You can get the general picture. And that's only in my own plane. There are also other aircraft flying at high speeds that are totally beyond my control that could come suddenly from any direction as well. It's like sparring with five opponents at once. This was a time for literal "global awareness." Karate helped me with aircraft awareness, and being a pilot helped my karate awareness skills. Awareness is essential for the daily lives of everyone. Your life or the lives of your loved ones depend on it.

General Awareness:
Intensely Aware and Prepared

OF ALL CRITICAL MENTAL KARATE SKILLS, awareness is probably the most important. There are many stories in the literature on samurai lore where awareness is the highest order of martial skill. You can easily find them in books and DVDs, and especially in the ancient samurai stories about Musashi, and in movies like *The Seven Samurai* (an idea we borrowed to make our Western cowboy classic, *The Magnificent Seven*).

There are many stories with a scenario that usually goes something like this: A father wishes to leave his legacy and inheritance to his brightest and the most highly skilled, of his three sword-wielding, fighting expert sons. So he arranges for two or three skilled warriors to hide in a room in the darkness, while he sits on the opposite side of the room facing the only door, and beckons his sons to enter. He commands them to enter one at a time, and waves each closer to him to speak.

The first son walks in, the hidden warriors leap out, beating him mercilessly. He, for certain, is not the chosen one.

The second son in line thinks to himself, "What a dullard. I'll certainly win my father's approval by taking care of these fools!" So the second son leaps into the room and the hidden warriors pounce. He defiantly defeats them after a short but violent brawl. "Ha!" he says to his father, "You see I am the most skilled!"

Finally, the father motions for his third son to enter. The son confidently walks up to the open doorway, where he abruptly stops and smiles. The father waves impatiently for his son to enter immediately. His son refuses, just grins, and points to where each of his father's thugs are hiding in the dark. This third son demonstrated the highest level of skill in being alert and aware of his father's intentions and the location of the hidden bad guys.

The advantages of being so alert and aware that risk factors become minimized should be obvious. The point of that same story, brought forward to the present, is just as relevant as ever. When I started karate and discussions on awareness came up, it was never new and strange to me because my father and grandfather were both police officers. Growing up it was quite normal in restaurants for dad not to choose a chair with his back to a door. When I chose a much safer career as a high school educator, I thought things would be much different because, after all, I was just developing young minds. Then, over time, more than one student told me that I should hope they never caught me outside of the school building. I had been karate training for over a decade at the time so my radar was automatically turned up. Preparing aware, alert attitudes, and thinking habits (the aware karate spirit) was not at all new to me. Prepared razor-sharp alertness and intuitive skills can be as complicated as being on military patrol in a battle-torn country, or being a police officer who is clearing an apartment, or it can be as simple as you and I turning on outdoor lights before going out after dark to feed our dog or cat.

One of my favorite illustrations is one that Randall Hassell used in his self-defense discussions. "If you get in your car, and someone hiding in the backseat suddenly grabs you by the throat, what is the self-defense for that?" While the students are thinking about it, he says, "It's really very simple: Before you get into your car, look in the backseat, and if there is a mugger lurking there, don't get in!"

Situational Awareness

We have all read the legendary stories and seen the movies about the samurai's nearly clairvoyant sense of situational awareness. I personally received my first instruction on this when I was about five years old. As I mentioned earlier, my father was a police officer and would never sit with his back to a window in a restaurant or even at home. At nightfall, our curtains at home were promptly shut. Anytime we were at home, day or night, we locked our doors. Since my other five-year-old friends thought this was strange, I asked my father why we observed these strange rituals, which my friends thought were weird.

"Well son," he said, "I'm a police officer and have had to cause some bad guys to be sent to jail, and some of them promised to kill me as soon as they get out." These were things (situational awareness), he said, "That people often don't think about to defend themselves, but they should."

"So, if our doors are locked, and I sit facing doors and windows, they can't sneak up on us as easy." Even at five years, I got the point. (My dad was never known for sugar-coating things.) As for situational awareness, you don't have to be a samurai or a rocket scientist to understand the basics.

Broad and Infinite Awareness

Awareness needs to be universal (broad and infinite), not narrowly focused.

The most vulnerable victims are those that allow some seemingly unimportant thing, (what we sometimes jokingly call a "shiny object") captivate and preoccupy their attention. Study after study in prisons indicate that the most vulnerable victims are those that are preoccupied with something like arguing with children over cookies, texting while walking along, loading groceries in a car trunk in a dark parking lot, or those that are just utterly oblivious to their surroundings.

In the literature, Funakoshi relates stories of how after a practice, over a bowl of rice, he instructed his students on the proper way to eat with chopsticks, so as not to be caught unaware and have them thrust into their eyes, nose, throat, or brain unexpectedly. During a TV interview of a retired CIA agent, by a popular (and cocky) host, the interviewer asked the retired spy what was the easiest way to kill someone like him and with what exotic weapon of choice?

The agent smiled and said very quickly, "Oh, that's easy! I take a Number-2 pencil and shove it upwards through your jaw, between the bones, and into your brain. You die instantly."

"A Number-2 pencil is all you need? Just a Number-2 pencil?" Understandably, the clever host was too stunned to pursue the matter. There were no further questions on that topic.

The necessity for awareness has no limitations. Just like all karate training "has no limits", according to Funakoshi.

Chapter 19

Mind Like Water --- Mind Like the Moon

Mind Like Water *(Mizu No Kokoro)*

Be the tranquil spirit amid turmoil;
Be the eye of the hurricane.

ANOTHER TRADITIONAL FACET TO AWARENESS is *mizu no kokoro*, meaning "mind like water." In karate training we learn to see what things really are, not what they seem. Keeping our mind calm and clear like a high mountain pond enhances awareness and allows us to more accurately perceive what the threat actually is and in real time. A calm pond surface reflects all around it, without error. This allows you to react appropriately and instantly to the actual threat that is presenting itself. The analogy here is that if our mind is calm, like the quiet, calm surface of a pond, we can accurately see the threat, just as we can see our reflection in the calm surface of the water, like a mirror. If our mind is turbulent in a state of panic, our brain is like turbulent water and cannot reflect (perceive) accurately the threat. If the mind is turbulent and confused, it cannot respond swiftly and correctly.

Learn to maintain mental calmness with a tranquil spirit, especially facing violent aggression. We absolutely cannot be speculating about what an opponent may or may not do. Maintain a calm spirit and allow intuition to launch correct actions or reactions. Calmness, especially in the face of aggression is an absolute necessity.

According to Sensei Stan Schmidt, JKA 8th Dan, and Japan Karate Association Shihankai member, commenting on *Mizu No Kokoro* (Mind like water): "Judgmental thinking stops immediate awareness."

Your fighting spirit must be calm without pre-judgmental thinking. Then, like the accurate reflection of still water, your own immediate awareness is heightened and accurate. You are then more prepared to accurately perceive and catch the slightest hint of the start of aggression. If you have any unnecessary fears or thoughts, it will be like throwing rocks into your reflective pond. Perception and quick reactions will be clouded. You will be handicapped at perceiving your opponent's actions and your reactions may be inappropriate and late.

However, if our mind is calm like a still pond reflection, we can likewise better perceive what is actually happening in real time, so that with good training, we can react instantly and appropriately. Mentally, be calm inside, seeing everything equally, with unfocused vision. You "visually perceive" instead of actually focusing your eyes on any one thing. Notice the slightest twitch or opening in an opponent's defenses. Outside your body can be quite active with your body moving freely and fluidly, but inside you are still. You must react instantly to opportunity without hesitation. Your spirit is calm and quiet within, but potentially explosive, like TNT just before ignition.

A similar tactic can be quite useful as well. It's a "lulling" tactic. As a tactic to confuse your opponent, you can seemingly switch postures. Just for fun, experiment with it in partner training. Begin with your mind calm and body outwardly active. Carefully monitor your opponent's movements and intentions as he reacts to your actions. Remember, you are calm inside while active outside (the eye of the hurricane).

Then, you suddenly stop your body movement and outwardly relax. Your mind must still remain calm, but actively alert and as aware as a razor blade is sharp. Your opponent will respond to your apparent change in tactics, usually by pausing briefly like you have done. At the instant he relaxes, pauses, and exhales, you explode! You have caused him to lower his mental guard by seeming to do it first. Musashi called this strategy "hypnotizing your opponent."

Reflections: Shark Attack!

If you watched the movie *Jaws*, were you more "aware" the next time you waded out into the ocean? I was. Great White sharks have evolved for a few million years into the perfect predator. It's just what they do. Off the tip of South Africa, there is an island where seals lay around unsuspectingly, minding their own business, until they decide to go for a swim to cool off or to grab a snack. And when they do that, a couple tons of 15-foot great white sharks swim silently but explosively, torpedoing vertically upward from the dark depths, slamming into the unsuspecting seal who, an instant earlier, was totally unaware of the lurking, predatory freight train. With jaws gaping wide and teeth flared, the sharks ram the seals at about 30 miles per hour. It's one of the few places in the world to view this and it is quite popular on many TV nature shows…unless you are a seal.

Here's a lesson: A predator (shark or human) seeks to catch a victim by surprise and attack so fast and unexpectedly, so violently, and so unrelentingly that the victim has no chance to escape or counter.

No skills will help at all if you are caught unaware like this. Clearly, awareness is the most important skill above all. But if we are aware of danger, we can be trained to counter-attack so vigorously, so violently, that the attacker has no chance but to run away or be defeated. Awareness is the key. Then we can "be the consequence" for their actions and "not the victim."

A keen sense of awareness and correct response is learned from daily practice. Nakayama said, "After a long period of practice, we can move unconsciously, freely and properly." But what is a long period of practice?

Sensei Stan Schmidt said it simply, from the first karate book he ever read, the one that gave him his first inspiration to train: "The karate man trains every day."

Karate is a participation endeavor that can forge our physical skills and boost our spirit. "That which does not kill us, makes us stronger!"

Mind Like the Moon *(Tsuki No Kokoru)*

Be aware of all things equally, and all at once.

LIKE THE RAYS OF A FULL MOON, shining down upon the earth illuminating all things, you see, hear, smell, feel, and sense all that surrounds you. Use all of your senses and intuition. Be aware of all details from the smallest to the largest.

Do not let one thing take your attention more than another; those distractions are often purposely created to do so. We joke in class about holding up a set of car keys and we say, "Don't look at the shiny object!" The rays of the moon, like your awareness, see all things equally and miss nothing.

You must be aware of things equally, and from all directions.

This is one of the many awareness skills that are critical for survival. It represents a very practical concept. In its purest form, it means to sense everything.

Imagine that on a clear night with a full moon overhead, the light of the moon shines down equally upon everything, all at the same time. Whether you are facing an opponent, entering a crowded room, or walking alone down a street at night, you take in everything at once, just as the moonlight blankets the earth beneath equally.

It does not shine on one spot then another, then another. It focuses on no particular thing. It blankets everything softly. Your senses in this state of awareness take in everything large and small. Your vision is not focused; vision is blurred. Perception is wide; nothing escapes your attention. This is critical in order to sense danger in your environment. Simply put, you are aware of all. This in practical terms means you may have to react to surprise attacks from any direction. Accumulated karate training better prepares you to be aware of, perceive and react to multiple attackers. Kata and sparring with multiple attackers are a good means of skill set training for reacting to multiple dangers. There are no guarantees. Practicing to be aware of all going on around you and making maximum use of all of your senses and observation skills are absolutely essential. They are a prerequisite to being able to avoid or react to hidden dangers --- dangers that are often hidden in plain sight.

Awareness in Dojo Training

The dojo is a great place to begin awareness training. So the next time you are across from your sparring partner, here are a few awareness skills to work on. Try to keep your view of your opponent very wide, like the radar screen at an international airport. In my dojo, we do regular training for global awareness.

Let nothing get close to you that you did not perceive. Here is a global awareness exercise you can do at your very next sparring class to increase your global sensory and your intuitive counter-attack skills. Your partners will not know you are doing it. You will be amazed at your immediate results. Pretend your eyes are about a foot above and behind your head, looking down on your situation and your opponent from above. Gaze forward toward (and through) your partner's throat area so you can see everything he does. Do not focus your eyes on any one thing even for a second. This will much improve your ability to perceive everything that endangers you and improves your response to the attacks. Sense your *ma-aii* (distance) and keep it safely to your advantage. Do not let your opponent creep into your space. If you allow your opponent to close in on you, your perception becomes narrowly focused, and your field of vision becomes "tunneled" and narrow. If you allow your mind to be focused or stuck on one thing, according to most martial arts masters, your ability to react quickly and appropriately to a threat becomes paralyzed. This is an extreme weakness; it leaves you with a mental opening that most certainly will be used against you. Keep your mind "unattached" and mentally aware of everything at once. Do these things across from a sparring opponent, in a fight for your life, driving to work, and for a walk in the park.

Awareness in spirit, an alert clear mind, is always good…always…always.

Chapter 20

The Beginner's Mind

THERE IS A CRITICAL COMPONENT LINK of both learning and teaching in karate, and in that order. The old analogy to humility in this case is, if we can keep the "beginner's mind," then we are always in the process of learning. Also, along those lines is the comparison to a cup of tea. If we are the empty cup, more tea can always be added. If the cup is always full (full of an over-sized ego), then no new tea (knowledge) can be added. When we are not learning from those around us, then we must try our best to take something, learn something, from all life experiences and observations around us, every day.

Remember that in karate, and we are always karate students, *there are no limits.* Most senior black belts that have trained for decades are pretty humble in this respect, because they know and appreciate how much they don't yet know.

Sensei Randall Hassell often explained it this way at black belt exams, comparing learning to a pyramid:

When we began to train, we were faced with a very broad range of things to learn, and they seemed to be spread out all around us, like the fat bottom of a pyramid. Then, as we climbed through the ranks and learned more, we consolidated and refined our knowledge, and as we climbed up the pyramid, there seems to be less and less that we didn't know. The higher up we climbed, it seemed, the lesser the amount of knowledge there was left, just as the pyramid narrows as we get closer to the top. Finally, after several years of work, we reach the top of the pyramid, which is first degree black belt (shodan). Then, at that point, when we reach this pinnacle of basic learning, so to speak, we look up toward higher degrees of learning, and we begin to see what we don't yet know.

Then we realize that there is another pyramid of knowledge standing point-to-point, upside-down, with the one we just climbed, forming an hour-glass. The new upside-down pyramid represents new and ever-expanding knowledge and growth that opens to us until the day we die.

We realize that just as we thought we had filled our cup, it is now empty again. But that is a good thing. Those that think they know it all are usually the type who came into the dojo with an inflated opinion of themselves. They usually quit soon. Others may reach a higher level of rank, or maybe they've won a tournament or two, and they think they now know it all. Often, they will quit as well. They burn brilliantly (in their own opinion), like a match, and then fizzle out like a match, very quickly. They are legends in their own minds.

Often karate shows what kind of person we are very quickly because every class is challenging. As challenges are faced, and because new learning in the dojo is always the norm, personality traits reveal themselves rather quickly. At any level of experience, you are grappling with every learning experience to get the most out of it. If you are the teacher (sensei or sempai) presenting the techniques or concepts, then you understand very quickly (often a quite pleasant surprise), that at the same time you are teaching, you are learning much more than your students. This is the correct spirit to view learning and teaching. Learn from everything possible.

If your mindset is in a lifelong-learning mode, you are in superb company. All of the most skilled senior instructors are constantly learning from each other, their students, their seniors, and every other source of information they can get their hands on. Even the great samurai swordsman like Miyamoto Musashi, learned not only from his battles, but also from spiritual experiences, mentors like the monk Takuan Soho, who taught him to control his wild spirit.

As a good student of karate, you must immerse yourself in as many experiences as you can with an open mind. As an instructor, you must build lessons that cause students to experience concepts, techniques, tactics, strategies, and the like.

Forgive mistakes and encourage bravery. The best lessons often come from mistakes.

As a student (kohai or sempai) or instructor (sensei), you must always express a towering determination to never give up, forging ahead, always be first a student and both leader and mentor, but at the very same time be tempered with humility and glowing with credibility. Because others will follow your lead and mirror your example, this is an honor and serious responsibility in karate-do.

Be a Lifelong Learner

Always be a karate student first, then an instructor. Remember, "sensei" means "teacher" and also, "one who has gone before." Think about it. To be a good teacher you must have been a good student first and foremost. And then, you can teach others to be good students so that eventually and hopefully, they will in turn become instructor, some day. Teach them to be lifelong learners in all things.

Always Keep "The Beginners Mind."

Chapter 21

Lone Wolf: Accept Responsibility
"Own It!"

WHEN YOU THINK ABOUT IT, karate appears to be a group activity. Chances are, you would join a class of students all doing nearly the same thing: blocks, punches, kicks, or kata, especially when you are first starting out. You may have the best instructor, the best equipment, the prettiest dojo, the biggest gym, and an abundance of information and reference materials.

But know this: Odds are that if you ever are attacked and have to use your training to survive, you will be alone. Violent criminals do not choose to attack groups of twenty; they like to single out the weak and alone. They would prefer that their victims are isolated and not able to get help, weak or helpless to make their job easier, and in a location with no witnesses. Consequently, when you are learning, teaching, and training, even though skill-building starts in a group class setting, train with the intensity and mindset like it is you, alone against the world.

This brings us full circle to Osamu Ozawa's strong advice on training with the intensity to convince your training partners that they are really going to be hit.

It is important that you do not depend on only the regular class environment for polishing and internalizing you skills. You must be motivated to initiate much personal practice on your own. Ultimately, you need be able to rely on only what you know on your own. Your life literally depends on it.

For every class in the dojo, you need another hour of practice alone. We are a nation and culture of "blamers." If you are attacked, impulse may tempt you to blame your sensei or your style of martial art for letting you down. Enjoy your classes with your friends and peers because humans are social animals, and that is good. But also train like the "lone wolf who prowls" with the higher purpose of discovering and increasing hidden potentials.

You need to be responsible for your own accomplishments. There is a legend about Musashi giving proper credit and seeking help from the gods. At the threshold of a temple, he stopped short of asking the gods for help in upcoming battles. From then on, he felt that one should respect one's god(s), but when it comes to combat with lives in the balance, you must depend on your own training.

Likewise, you cannot depend on the police to save you, and you will not always have time to call 911. If, for example, a good police response time after the call is 15 to 20 minutes, and the average attack/self-defense time is two to four seconds, then you have some time to be accountable for until help arrives.

Ultimately, you alone are responsible for the internalization and use of your survival skills. If your training saves your life, or the life of a loved one, just one time, it would be well worth your best effort. Train hard!

Chapter 22

Sensei with a "Student-Centric" Spirit

THOSE WHO GIVE BACK are remembered and respected for their contributions and leadership. Karate knowledge expands and its contributions to humanity multiply. If one becomes a tournament champion, or a "big shot black belt" (term learned from Shihan Osamu Ozawa), and learns much, but then if that knowledge is not shared with others, then what good is it? The term "sensei" does not imply learning skills but not sharing, nor passing them along. Karate would never had gotten to us all in the wonderful quality that it has, if senseis in the past had been selfish and not passed it along. It would not continue to evolve and improve as it does.

We must share our knowledge and "give back" to improve our martial arts. If you willingly share with your students and, teach them, they will become skilled, and the quality of your martial art will improve. As an instructor, the goal must be to make each student the best they can be. Help them realize their potentials.

Like a sculptor looks at the block of granite and sees a vision of a work of art that is locked hidden inside, look at beginners and in your mind's eye, see future black belts. The goal must be to lead, inspire, and teach them to be better than you. Of course, many will quit and disappoint you. On the other hand, don't be too discouraged. Eventually, especially if you are a good instructor, often students will eventually pass you up. After all, if you are a good instructor, this is your goal.

Organizationally Speaking

Karate is people-centered. Rather than cranking out marketing schemes that would make Wall Street proud, let your organization grow and mirror the quality of karate instruction you've given and the credibility you've earned.

Be student-centric. If you invest quality instruction into your students, your club and organization will grow naturally and strongly from inside-outward. Put your efforts into making each student the best they can be. Make them surprise even themselves.

CHAPTER 23

Makiwara: Anvil of Spirit Training

The Punching Post

YOU FACE THE MAKIWARA, the punching post, in an anchored stance; cracked, bloodied, calloused knuckles punching. One, two, ten, a hundred! Hammering undaunted determination into the human spirit-energy, power, thought, and the soul merge with truth. Focus, kime, no-thought, merge with the punching post!

One, two, twenty, two hundred, five hundred. Ironically, the more you relax at the beginning and throughout most of your punch, the faster the technique is, and the more energy and impact force is transferred in the last instant.

The more you relax during the technique properly, the more kinetic energy is formed and the more the impact shock wave is transfer into the makiwara, your imaginary opponent. But the makiwara becomes your friend and it's hard to walk past it without the urge to hit it. Whack! Physical feedback is in the shock wave felt on impact and the sound like a clap of thunder. Impact force is cleanly delivered. If not, you know by the sound and the feel. If you are making an incorrect fist, for example, you will know instantly. All the small things you learn or teach suddenly come together for real, there is no "fudge factor." You'll know the truth of your technique, good or bad.

The punching post fosters tenacity, correct timing and tension, expansion and contraction, breathing, and strengthens the determined, controlled spirit. It is the "anvil" that hammers the spirit and technique into one.

The makiwara is more of the consistency of tough bone and tissue than modern softer bags. Your true goal of the makiwara is *ikken hissatsu,* killing with one technique. If you are attacked by multiple attackers you are not fighting ten rounds, you are eliminating one attacker with lethal force.

We asked Hirokazu Kanazawa once how often, or how many punches, we should practice a day. He said, "When you are young and learning, you can do hundreds, but when you get older and your techniques are stronger but your body is more in risk of damage, 30-40 is plenty."

Applying High-Spiritedness for Maximum Effect

With the makiwara punching post, we practice how to apply high-spirited techniques using the punching post as our stubbornly immovable opponent. We learn how to relax and mentally focus. We learn to blend and use our mental and physical technique components for maximum effect. The audible "thud" and the vibration we feel coming back from the post to us monitors our progress. We are practicing the process of combining our fighting spirit and our technique. We are tuning up the "how" to apply our best potential.

In our discussions of initiative --- *sen* --- think about this: each time we wind up and punch the makiwara, we are pulling the trigger on our best effort, and with a big *kiai,* we fuel our punch with fighting spirit. Along with proper breathing and the synchronized firing of technique muscle groups, we hammer away. This, however, is still in reality against a post that does not move and try to kill you.

Now, let's look at the "when."

Against an aggressive opponent trying to destroy you, the "when" suddenly becomes all-important. Spirit training is "applied commitment" to the extreme. Commitment has very real power. But if it is applied uselessly at the wrong time, it can turn into misspent energy. Learning when to commit, and when it is the correct time to take the initiative in a volatile situation is critical. If you are trained to launch a highly energized counter-attack at the perfect instant to achieve maximum results, you become a very dangerous person to be reckoned with.

Taking the initiative is all about understanding when it is best to be poised, and when it is best to open the floodgates of all of your combined martial skills.

Sensei Stan Schmidt often tells a short story of the harmless looking mongoose killing the mighty king cobra. You will find actual footage in his DVD, *The Winning Blow*. Just watch; no further explanation is needed. The mongoose has perfect timing; he is immersed in fighting spirit, and blindingly fast technique. He is totally committed, and his life is on the line. Correct initiatives result in a happy mongoose with a full belly and a dead cobra. If he makes even a small mistake seizing the opportunity, taking the wrong initiative, miss-applying even his best high-spirited efforts, then there is a happy cobra.

Once you have developed your ultimate technique, using it at the correct time and place is everything.

Chapter 24

The Magic of "When" -- Taking the Initiative

IF YOUR LIFE IS ON THE LINE, understanding the all-important "when" and how to explosively unleash your high-spirited techniques, with a "fire in your belly," will make all the difference and can mean life or death.

Musashi, *Sen*, and When

Myamoto Musashi and his peers, during the 1600s in Japan, based much of their training on the concept of *sen* --- taking the initiative. It was considered a determining factor for survival in combat with life and death literally at stake.

These concepts, fundamental in karate, kendo, and all combative martial arts and self-defense, are essential.

In our Midwest karate programs, we have always taught and stressed the strong fundamentals advocated by Master Funakoshi and his peers. Karate basics are dependable when your back is against the wall because they stand up to the historic standards of budo that define authentic traditional karate internationally.

Determined hard and continuous training in karate should result in learning to take correct initiatives. Sen is critically significant in self-defense (life and death situations), in partner training, in tournament competition, and becoming more confident and comfortable applying *sen*, it can be used with other modern everyday issues in work and play as well.

In fact, properly taking initiatives is a fact of life all around us. We use *sen* driving each day, we use initiatives of all sorts and with different timing in jobs, and even in making investments in the stock market. If you are not aware of many types of taking initiatives, be assured that others are using them on you.

I once read a book review on one of several translations of Miyamoto Musashi's, *Book of Five Rings*. The wonderful review said that Musashi's strategies were often used in Japanese business competition in the marketplace. This seemed to make perfect sense, as I had read *The Book of Five Rings* several times, so, I decided to put the idea to a test. I wish I could brag that I personally made millions on the stock market, but, well, not so much. However, I happened to be in downtown Chicago, at the "Gold Coast," the "Million Dollar Mile," and walked into a book store, and went directly to the business section to conduct my test. Lo and behold, on the top shelf of a very classy selection of business and marketing publications, was *The Book of Five Rings* by Musashi. We encounter *sen* in one way or another, every day of our life. It is best to study and use it. One rule of the universe is that "if you are not in action, then you are being acted upon." Timing is everything.

Spirit training maximizes motivation, enthusiasm and commitment. It inspires actions with self-directed timing, and intensity. Using all this potential energy with a sense of timing and intensity is governed by our spirit training experiences. *Sen* is essential to correctly applying energized fighting spirit and using it with proper applications of pre-emptive action and reactions.

Sen No Sen and *Go No Sen*

Commonly, *sen no sen* is characterized as taking the initiative early, or attacking first, while, *go no sen* is characterized as taking the initiative later, or counter-attacking. However, go no sen is not simply counter-attacking. It is not merely waiting and then reacting to your opponent's attack. It is, in some respects, planning for your opponent's attack by actively or passively causing the opponent to attack in a manner that you want them to, so that you then can crush them with a counter-attack of your choice.

Experience, Treachery, and Sen

With years of karate training, I've learned that when to pull the trigger on taking the initiative is more important to me especially helpful as I get older. Experience, knowledge, and wisdom will give the expertise to find weak points and the right timing to act. Continuous karate training is always critical to have the abilities. I have to be more careful to restrain my "mind not making bills my body can't pay." There are great karate athletes with youth and strength who can overcome powerful opponents. I applaud them. Been there. Did that. In fact, I remember at clinics when I was younger of instructors telling us that we should not rely on our youth and speed. We should rely on the sound kinetics of using the karate techniques correctly because the real usefulness of karate is designed in technique. When we are no longer young and as strong as nature will demand, it will be the power generated by performing technique correctly that will save the day. In Funakoshi's autobiography he shares some karate he used as an elderly man against younger attackers that proved to be quite powerful and painful for his attacker.

Osamu Ozawa told us about being verbally assaulted by two would-be bad guys as they tried to steal his car as he was walking out of a store. He said one got too close to him, in his face, demanding his keys. Oops! Sensei Ozawa said he just slapped him in the face (that may have resembled a focused palm-heeled strike...just speculating) and the slap broke the young man's jaw. As the man lay writhing on the ground holding his jaw, his accomplice ran away. When the police questioned Ozawa, he truthfully said, "I just slapped him hard." He took his initiative simply and effective.

Now, as I have become older and must deal with my own joints naturally wearing out and the tissues slowing down; having a strong spirit, years working on decent basic karate skills, and using *sen* to my advantage are a saving grace. I can no longer dazzle opponents with youth and fancy footwork, so I must resort to "experience and treachery." Timing is everything. At times, I can only, as the old samurai saying goes, "Tense my belly and attack!" We all get older. And in self-defense, winning is not the most important thing, it's the only thing!

The importance of understanding sen, taking the initiative, is huge in self-defense, kumite, and other human endeavors. The how and the when is critical.

Taking the Initiative: Nuts and Bolts
To Think is to Die

The mind must be relaxed. Remember that to react intuitively, correctly and instantly to an attack, we absolutely cannot be mentally preoccupied and indecisive. The mind cannot be cluttered with demons of fear and "what ifs." or it will be paralyzed at the very time that actions should be instantly launched. We can train techniques to be nearly automatic, but we must learn to be calm, mentally serene. This is to quickly enter the mental state of *mushin* (no-mind), a theoretically "empty mind." This is not easily taught to students because if you tell them they must empty their mind, they will no doubt be "thinking" of what you said, defeating the purpose. If you tell someone NOT to think of a big black bear, they will be thinking of a big black bear. Creative instructors describe mushin, not thinking, and then come up with drills to help. It's just something that is experienced with success, and then that feeling is recaptured until it becomes easy to attain on command. If training is repeated until karate techniques are embedded into the subconscious as described by Nakayama and Nishiyama, this whole process comes together very well. If the conscious mind is thinking about all the fears and concerns a dangerous situation might present, it is just not fast enough to react. An attacker will not let you have time to think. Milliseconds become precious.

Interception

Awareness continually reappears as a critical skill. This interception concept involves taking the initiative to attack your opponent when he is about to attack, or even when he is even thinking of attacking. Realizing how well this works is often like looking in a mirror at yourself to be sure you are not giving away openings for an opponent to see. In fact, using actual mirror training to practice your starting movements can help you see openings that you may be telegraphing, while understanding how to apply this interception technique on others. Put this into your "secret training" tool box for homework. I digress.

The concept of interception begins with being extremely attentive to your opponent. Watch very closely (gaze, don't focus your eyes) to sense even the slightest hint of movement. Gazing toward the throat area, attack at the first "twitch" of his facial, throat or shoulder muscles. Do not wait until you have been hit to be convinced of danger or you could lose. Be aware of breathing patterns, the slightest twitch of a muscle, or even the veins in the neck. It's impossible for a human to move toward you without contracting or moving something. Training to perceive that initial movement is the key. Attack explosively, with no thought or hesitation. Attack his attack, in the very first millisecond of its initiation. Do not wait. We popularly call this "interception" training. Students enjoy training drills that sharpen these perceptions and reactions, and they enjoy success very quickly. Move in swiftly with a confident spirit, keeping a good posture, balanced, hips low, and using your hip power with techniques. If, then, an opponent becomes off-balance, or retreats, don't give them a chance to recover; be relentless.

Attack at the First Sign of Attack

Legally speaking, in most states in the U.S., one needs only to truly fear that lives are in immediate danger to justify a strong counter-attack. In karate we understand that it is important not to wait to see what technique was coming before reacting. If we do, we are too late. It is much better to be alive, to sort it out all in court later, than to be dead. Pre-program with good continuous karate training that is reinforced with regular practice. In real life, we should also assume the opponent may have a concealed weapon and if we wait to see what it is, we lose. A bad guy may wish to distract you with an attack and has a couple friends hiding in-wait, out of sight. Do not hesitate. When required, commit to an attack mentally and physically with explosive power. It's best to rely on your strongest, most effective basic techniques. Awareness is your best friend again.

The Distant Gaze:
Blurred Vision and a Crystal-Clear Mind

Facing an opponent, we ideally keep a mind clear of thoughts and our vision blurred. An empty mind is not likely in practical terms, but not letting thoughts become "stuck" on any one thing or distracted is important. If in karate kumite, a partner says, "Look! Your shoe's untied!" I'm certain that you would not look down. Remaining calm, on alert and observant is crucial.

I encourage students to gaze toward the mountain or ocean a hundred miles off in the distance, looking "through" their opponent's throat area, and far behind them as if staring off to the horizon. This helps give a global perception where their attention is on everything at once. If the eyes are not focused on anything, less escapes attentiveness and it's easier to perceive the start of any motion. "Mind like the moon" again, seeing everything equally all at once. It's an idea like the control tower at a busy airport, with vision and constant radar "seeing" hundreds of aircraft at once, and the operators in the tower are ready to spring into action. Your gaze should me your own radar and enable you to do the same.

Mental Openings

When your opponent is thinking about what he is going to do to you, sizing you up, maneuvering around to gain an advantage, then he is mentally open to attack. As he is trying to make his decision, his mind is indecisive or preoccupied: this is a mental opening. Attack with commitment. This first requires the high levels of awareness that are discussed above and requires much practice. Think of the old saying about "becoming one with your opponent." In other words, you can almost "feel" when your opponent's mind is occupied. He cannot think about defending against your attack, at the same time he is planning to attack you. It's kind of like holding up a shiny coin and saying, "Look at the shiny object!" When he looks (theoretically speaking), you explode and attack! This is a mental opening and a tactical opportunity for you to take advantage of. When you sense any such mental indecision, go. This just takes a lot of practice and learning from mistakes. Let's face it, until you get the hang of it, you will make mistakes. Welcome to karate! But that's what dojo training is all about. It's a safe, controlled environment for us to live through mistakes. Eventually, we all learn. Things will start to click.

If it's difficult to tell when your kumite partner is thinking of what to do, you might show an opening (and be a little too far away to be touched), then suddenly switch the opening you show; then attack right away. While his mind must switch to aim for your new opening, you can capitalize on his momentary indecision. Caution: the more skilled your partner is, the less time it will take for him to adjust. Have an attentive and explosive spirit!

Learning Initiative --- the Hard Way

When I was a student at Illinois State University, we had we had a fairly large karate tournament. All the teams from several states proudly paraded in, holding banners high with team names, just like in Japan. I still remember that the music blasting over the speakers as we filed in was the theme to the movie, *The Good, the Bad, and the Ugly*. Nothing says an outstanding traditional Japanese karate tournament like the theme song from a Clint Eastwood Spaghetti Western. Although, as I looked around the gymnasium at our motley looking competitors, the title, "The Good, the Bad, and the Ugly" seemed to be fitting, almost inspiring.

It was a hurry-up-and wait process, as most tournaments in those days were. Finally, my division came up. I was a brand-new Shodan, and I was pumped. I won my first three or four matches, and my confidence was soaring. My next opponent was a black belt from Kentucky with a dozen years of training.

He wasn't extremely big in stature and not very intimidating to me. Notice that I "pre-judged" my opponent and assumed that his non-threatening demeanor meant he might not be a problem for me; not a smart way of thinking at all. This was an old fashioned traditional tournament, so one full point would win the match. But it had to be a high-quality technique.

"*Hajime!*" said the center judge, and I charged in with high-spirited *kias* and a flurry of punches and kicks. No points scored, but I drove him out of the ring.

Several times I charged in fearlessly, and my opponent retreated and blocked. I was feeling invincible (mistake) and having great fun charging him around the ring. Suddenly, I scored a half point punching to his face, and my confidence soared. This was going very well, and I knew all I needed was just one more half point.

We returned to our starting line and bowed to each other courteously.

I was an instant legend in my own mind. "*Hajime!*" the referee yelled, and the fight was on. I confidently stepped forward to settle down solidly into my sparring stance. I would ready myself to launch another flurry of techniques and proceed to get my next half point and win this match. I was just a half-point away.

(Note: pick out some things above that I should not have been thinking about at all.)

BAM! To my great surprise, and before the soles of my feet could grip the floor, I had two hard knuckles and a fist buried in my chest. This was truly a deer in headlights moment. "*Yame!*" cried the judge.

How could happen? I didn't even get to assume my very strong stance, and there was an *oizuki* hammering me dead center. "*Ippon!*" said the judge. "Match!" he said, as he waved his hand sharply toward my opponent. "Scoring with *oizuki*. Your opponent (me) caught off balance (sleeping) and making no attempt to block."

My opponent caught me "sleeping" with a basic straightforward and very fast lunge-punch. I had shown him a huge mental opening. My mind was locked onto thoughts of what could have been. I should not have been thinking at all; I should have been aware and attentive from the command to begin. He noticed that each time I started, I stepped forward to get settled for just a second (a huge amount of time in a match) before I charged. It was a classic "interception" taking advantage of my "mental opening." My sempai had given me a valuable lesson.

I've learned many more lessons from getting hit because of mistakes than probably anything else. I've taught students since then to be defensively alert to even the smallest things, and ways to intercept attacks with counter-attacks. Most memorable, I learned that, "It isn't over 'til it's over!"

When we think too much, we just get into trouble. There is no time to think in sparring and combat. Be aware at all times. Small things can be extremely critical.

Making Use of Openings in Breathing Patterns

Be aware of an opponent's breathing patterns. Typically, attacks (especially strong ones) are preceded with an inhaling breathing pattern. This is quite natural human behavior because oxygen is required in the muscles used to perform techniques. If possible, use your heightened state of awareness to sense your opponent's breathing patterns. Attack at the lowest part of the breathing pattern as exhalation has nearly emptied your opponent's lungs of air. Time your attack to the lowest oxygen level, the bottom of your opponent's breathing pattern.

We all inhale in preparation to exert a technique or any other large physical effort. This is a natural human function that precedes strong actions. If possible, attack strongly and repeatedly. Don't allow even a short pause for the opponent to recover their breath. If you have been moving about and exchanging techniques to test each other, breathing patterns are easier to perceive. This is a "karate secret," but I loved to get across from someone, in training drills, who I knew ahead of time smoked cigarettes heavily, because their breathing patterns became evident a little more quickly. Be in a spirit of high–alertness, miss nothing, and keep your mind clear. You must allow your subconsciously stored (internalized) techniques to launch at the bottom of your opponent's breathing pattern. However, you must be on guard because your breathing patterns are being watched as well.

CHAPTER 25

Kuzushi: Upsetting Your Opponent's World

CRUSH THE OPPONENT'S STABILITY AND POSTURE and upset their world. The feeling of the Shotokan Kata, Basai Dai, is general described as that of "storming a fortress." This is a very similar feeling to the principle of *kuzushi*: destabilizing your opponent and crushing his balance. Figuratively speaking, while storming the fortress is the spirit in Basai Dai, like mashing the walls down, you could think of the same feeling associated with *kuzushi* as swiftly "bringing the house down." The purpose here is not merely scoring a punch or kick, although we do that after unbalancing our opponent. The purpose of *kuzushi* is to upset the opponent's stability with unbalancing techniques, overpowering them with a crushing feeling in order to to disorient, and to confuse; demoralizing their spirit.

Like most things karate, any time we can sense weakness, inattention, hesitation, or the like, is a good time to attack. In kuzushi, sense the opponent's timing, keep the hips low and slide into a position to apply a jolting sweeping or throwing technique, accompanied by a finishing attack. In doing so, apply power with the spirit of being a freight train. As balance is destroyed, instantly apply a follow-up punch or other technique to finish the process. If it wasn't enough to rattle your opponent's spirit by turning them head over heels, then totally deflate whatever may be left with a finishing blow. Destabilizing the opponent, destroying balance, and totally rattling his cage is kuzushi. Do not allow them to regain composure, balance and momentum. Keep them down with high-spirited dominance. On the street especially, assume that if he gets up, he will use a knife or gun on you. This is especially important if it's understood that this opponent can be stronger, more skilled, better armed than you and may have friends near.

Scoring points alone is flawed training for survival

Thinking of scoring points for matches is fine for competition practice. In most competition, "extra-credit" is given for scoring with a punch, for example, while the punch is applied with a sweep that crushes the opponent's stability. If you can test techniques in a full-speed timed match experience against an unknown opponent, it will certainly help judge the effectiveness of your kuzushi weapons.

Training for real world application where no referee will say stop, requires thinking about different environments, footing, clothing, lighting, etc. Playing tag with punches, kicks, and strikes is not really kuzushi. While helpful in learning technique use, out of a more serious feeling for crushing an attacker so that they cannot come back into action is crucial. It should be understood by students that street application requires a more serious feeling. The stakes are just too high for anything less.

Many excellent programs address the need for more serious realism on the street. Sensei James Hartman, a 6th Dan in Shotokan, has been a defensive tactics and firearms instructor for the Peoria, Illinois Police Department for over 25 years. He regularly teaches all sorts of kuzushi tactics to police officers who have to diffuse threats and nullify aggressors routinely. He has infused many karate tactics into the police curriculum combine with other tactics to be used with aggressors of all sorts, armed and unarmed, often breaking up fights and altercations between two or more people who are in a violent rage against each other as well. He has taken his police street-defensive tactic training and his karate training and created a wonderful "Fight Back" Program in the dojo for women. The accent is on basic karate, other street appropriate tactics, kuzushi, and a bight shot of fighting spirit training to empower women to overcome physical attackers. One of the favorite drills is using the padded "red suit" worn by one of our other "volunteer" instructors. Upon being attacked by the padded intruder, the ladies, of all ages and sizes, are taught and encouraged, cheered on, to unbalance, knock down, and strike and kick the "perp," until they could not reasonably recover. The class clearly brings out the best in fighting spirit that the ladies didn't know they had in them.

Kuzushi is a critically important skill to have in your empty-hand arsenal, especially when there may be only a brief second of opportunity against overwhelming odds, a strong opponent, a bad guy on the street, multiple attackers, or against an opponent with a weapon. Your spirit has to be determined and committed to disorienting, unbalancing, and crushing your opponent's aggression.

Kuzushi: *crush the opponent's stability and spirit and do not let them recover.*

CHAPTER 26

Mushin: The Higher Stage

MU: nothing / SHIN: mind --- MUSHIN: "empty mind"

ACCORDING TO MARTIAL ART EXPERTS throughout history, during individual combat and especially in cases of surprise attack, the ability to react instantly and correctly with no time to think, subconsciously, is a higher order skill that is needed for survival. This is a state of mind void of thoughts of panic, evaluation, or indecision; it is when training takes over. If you have to think about what to do, those thoughts impair reaction time and slow the use of the techniques that are needed to use to respond appropriately.

If you are thinking about *mushin*, you are not doing it. We have to train properly so that we are able to react without thinking. As stressed earlier, a clear mind allows our subconscious mind to instantly perceive the danger and react as the situation dictates. If our mind is cluttered with thoughts of fear, like "Oh my goodness I'm going to be hurt or killed!" or "I wonder which techniques could save my life?", or, "Where's my phone? I have to dial 911!" then valuable time is wasted in deliberations when you need to take immediate action. It's like going on autopilot or instantly getting "in the zone."

Training for Mushin

We are trained in traditional karate to practice techniques repeatedly and correctly. Karate is a lifetime pursuit. If you are a 19-year-old, you may tend to feel that even if you are doing techniques incorrectly, you can make up for the sloppy technique because you are strong and fast. You may be right to a point. But you are not going to be young and strong forever. The beauty of authentic traditional karate styles are that the power of each technique results from the design and correct use of the human body. The mind and body are trained together in an inseparable scientific manner. This is why smaller people can be quite devastating against larger people. Older, weaker people can be just as powerful as younger and stronger, but less skilled people. Power and function come mostly from correct performance of the karate technique. In this respect, karate becomes a great equalizer.

The important point is, train correctly. Add layer upon layer of skill sets in basics (kihon), applications (kumite), and formal self-training for applications of many varieties of fundamentals and advanced combinations and tactics (kata). In general, the more repetitions we do, sometimes to the point of obsession, the more technique patterns are fed into our subconscious mind. These can be accessed later without having to think first. Indecision can get you killed.

All training must be correct training. Your mind is like the finest computer ever built. If you put enough good information in, then you can retrieve good information back out. If you put junk in, you get junk back out. Good training creates quality karate response patterns that can be drawn from your subconscious mind without hesitation. Funakoshi called this "internalization."

This level of skill is the mark of a dedicated martial artist. A recreation-oriented student will not achieve these results. You must decide which you are. Instructors must determine which of these class expectations dictate. Children's classes or

short-term self-defense classes obviously require different emphasis on training outcome expectations. Age and maturity require different adaptations and curriculum. Topics like mushin should probably be reserved for the long-term, serious-minded, competitive, mature, and possibly instructor destined students. That's a karate instructor's call.

Mushin allows correct intuitive response. This is essential because intellect becomes useless, and even obstructs our ability to use the skills we have acquired through cumulative training.

Making our mind blank is probably impossible because you won't know when a surprise attack will come. It will no doubt take a second or more to realize what is happening. Your attacker has decided, through treachery that he will not give you any time, not even a second, to think and evaluate the danger and decide what to respond with. That is why it is called a surprise! Your salvation is in years of training and repetition. Practice so that you can act accordingly, even when you do not have the luxury of time to sort things out. Michael Jordan did not become great in basketball by having to ponder which basket he needed to make next. Years and years and millions of baskets resulted in his amazing legendary hoop skills. Without thinking he left spectators spellbound as he flew through the air to cram the ball in and score.

Acting with *mushin*, intuitively, is a response method that has been polished in the martial arts for millennia. In old times, it was a life or death necessity. It is equally necessary for and practiced (whether by name or not) by today's modern warriors. For example, Navy Seals and special ops groups, fighter pilots, on down to the basic foot soldiers and emergency medical responders, all train with a high attention to details until their actions are automatic, even in the fog of war. In some technical areas of expertise, new generations of warriors, who were reared on computer games, are found to have an advantage in operating highly technical warfare triggering devices with computerized range-finding, aiming, and firing mechanisms.

In fact, *mushin* and, similarly, "moving zen" (keeping your mind unattached in a life and death environment) are applied in emergency response and rescue teams, firefighting and law enforcement responses. Calm, cool and collected is the desired mental state while moving swiftly to save lives.

Reflections

I recently was in a medical emergency myself that required my entrance as a patient into a hospital emergency department. The collective presence of *mushin* seemed to be in that ER. Once I was wheeled in, the emergency response team, surgeon, and all other medical staff in their respective fields of expertise, moved like a finely tuned machine all around me. On this occasion, my own life was on the line. I probably appreciated their level of skill more than the average person, because I truly understood and valued what I was seeing. Experienced doctors were acting intuitively and very quickly, and thank goodness, correctly.

> *"After a long period of practice, we can move unconsciously, freely, and properly."*

Intuition is defined as the power of knowing things without consciously thinking of them. In other words, your technical knowledge is stored in the subconscious. You can access the knowledge from your years of training and without the need to think about it. Training to intuitively perform appropriate and precise responses to attack (and other emergencies) is the highest stage of development for any skill set.

But don't take my word for it; let's see what some of the greatest martial art experts say: Referring to the "highest stage," Masatoshi Nakayama said, "After a long period of practice, we can move unconsciously, freely, and properly."

Seeing the opponent's actions and responding appropriately should be "a single momentary act," said Hidetaka Nishiyama, in *Karate, The Art of Empty Hand Fighting*. "Mind directed reflexes don't have time to 'think' what to do."

In the 1600s, Takuan Soho (a mentor to Miyamoto Musashi) says in *The Unfettered Mind*, that after much training the "arms and legs remember what to do" without the need for conscious thinking.

According to Sensei Randall Hassell, in *The Karate Experience: A Way of Life*, "We practice until our techniques become second nature… emanating from the unconscious, or from the original mind. It is the state of mind of the spider spinning its web."

Dr. Lester Ingber said, in *Karate Kinematics and Dynamics* that in highly skilled disciplines like karate, exact body techniques are practiced nearly to obsession. The execution and timing of these techniques "is expressed at the subconscious level" where, due to proper dedicated training, the "intuitions and pattern flows have become" a natural "part of the decision-making process."

Through repeated and correct training over long periods of time, correct intuitive responses are saved into your subconscious mind. In fact, scientists have just recently discovered eight new levels of the subconscious mind that can be packed with techniques, tactics, strategies, and other nearly limitless information.

The karate secret here is training, training, and more training!

Thoughts of indecision, fear, and technique choices, will only clutter your mind and get in the way of you doing the right thing in the face of extreme danger. Train correctly, cohesively, and with dedication. Be as natural as the spider spinning its' web.

Like many things involved in spirit training, *mushin* is very real but not obvious until it is used. If you have seen the movie, *The Last Samurai,* Tom Cruise's character is advised that his swordsmanship will improve if he can eliminate thought. Once he learns to clear his mind (only a few scenes later with Hollywood magic) he can quickly kill half a dozen sword-swinging attackers all by himself. It is a bit over the top, but the point is well made.

Mushin is not "smoke and mirrors." It works as an open gateway for heightened awareness and intuitive action. It is a state of mind that is close to be a "void." Conscious thinking is not allowed to interfere with unconscious karate action.

Chapter 27

Practicing Karate Do and the Ghosts of Budo

You've have probably heard and read accounts of new students entering a dojo, and after a class or two, asking the head instructor how long it would take to get a black belt. And the instructor's response was to reach in a drawer, pull out a black belt, and say, "Here you go, that will just be five bucks." The puzzled student, often stuttering and stumbling for words, usually rephrases by asking how long it might take before one can attain a high enough skill level to earn a black belt. The instructor is making the point that karate is much, much more than "getting the belt." But let's consider some of the other implications and the significance of wearing a traditional uniform and strapping on a black belt.

Implications of Dan Ranking

Black belt has been a symbol of achievement and power. But more than that, it has an historic legacy and even an aura of credibility and wisdom. For a holder of a black belt rank, it is intolerable not to honor the generations of sacrifice, blood and sweat of your predecessors in Budo.

One must accept the responsibility to show attributes of fighting spirit combined with integrity. Exemplary character are goals to strive toward for karate students and are outlined, for example, in *Dojo Kun* (dojo codes of behavior) and many other karate precepts that raise the bar on karate-appropriate attitudes, behaviors, and actions for serious students of karate-do. These different qualities must be combined in the personality and character of the human being awarded the black belt levels. Even if the experienced karate student has superior fighting skills far above an average black belt level, without daily work toward positive character development, they will not be up to par for carrying the mantle of Dan-level that our karate founders intended. Of course, we cannot perfect something that will never be perfected because we are all human. But we just must keep plugging away and try. It's the not-giving-up that counts. We are always a work in progress.

The Ghosts of Budo

So, with those thoughts and perspectives in mind, every time I put on my uniform, I get the uneasy feeling that the ghosts of a thousand years of Budo are looking over my shoulder, auditing my commitment to be vigilant and toward a more virtuous level of integrity and behavior.

Get Out of Your Comfort Zone

Karate conduct, strengths, and attitudes, as taught by Funakoshi and his peers, is not only practiced in the confines of the dojo but is also incredibly useful in other areas in of life. Most important concepts of karate training force us to push out of our comfort zone to obtain extraordinary growth.

Built into the karate-do practices are learning new techniques and applying them in combative, stressful situations. This teaches us to face all sorts of challenges with commitment, self-assurance, and positive thinking. We are forced by our sensei to quickly overcome inertia and apathy because our lives may depend on it. We learn through karate that goals can be set, worked toward, and accomplished through our own initiatives and effort. We learn to focus our mental and physical energies and direct them like lasers toward desired outcomes.

Accomplishments in all areas of our lives give more self-satisfaction, encouragement, and the self-confidence that we can build on for future success. It's like the old saying, "Success breeds success."

If you can use the principles outlined in the paragraph above in your life, then you will have a greater sense of who you are, and you will build stronger skill sets including the courage to focus energies to accomplish many of the things that will make life happier and more fulfilling. You will know in your heart that you have the power to meet seemingly impossible challenges that life has to offer and succeed.

Patience Training

It's easy in our digital world to become impatient. We crave faster laptops, so we can work on tasks we are creating, check our email, and chat at the same time we may be watching DVDs, texting on our phone, and all while we are eating fast food... We learn impatience. Things should happen at the same blinding speed that our fingers hit the keyboard, touch the screen, or we use voice commands!

We easily forget the patience to enjoy a beautiful sunset, take a walk through the woods, learn a musical instrument, go for a bike ride, or just to read a good book and enrich our lives --- just to "smell the roses." It's no wonder new students want that first belt tests the week after they sign up. Society teaches impatience. We forget that the quality of our journey is most important. Enjoying each training session is far more important worrying about how soon you can change belt colors.

I remember my first official "patience training." It came sitting in *seiza*, on our bent knees, sitting back on our heels, for the first time. "Sit back! Straighten up! Close your eyes and rest your palms on your legs quietly! Breathe calmly! I know it hurts but this is a patience exercise!" our instructor shouted. Each second seemed like an hour so clearly, he was right. Other times our class would be practicing kicks while standing on one leg, holding our kicking legs straight out. We were all drenched in sweat, teetering in a semi-balanced state, and groaning. Our instructor would slowly walk around making corrections while our veins nearly exploded with effort. When he sensed we were about ready to collapse, he forbade us any relaxation, and would slowly walk around the room whistling a slow tune.

"Patience exercise everyone!" he would smile and say. I confess that I passed these little "joys" onto my own students. Being patient enough to struggle through adversity to reach higher goals is just part of karate training.

No particular organization really has claim to the world-patent on karate

There has been somewhat of an evolution. Once a handful of organizations promoted themselves as the only place to get "real" karate. Today, we have progressed to a time where organizations are a vehicle for like-minded people to gather for deeper karate study and research, to improve whatever style of karate or martial art they practice. In other words, dedicated quality karate study is the main purpose of the organization and the goals are based on the benefits of the students. This has been the case with our Central Illinois Shotokan Karate Association from the beginning in the 1970s. Students come first, and our organizations have always been the vehicle to bring the best traditional karate training possible to them. It is within the framework of our organizations that good karate study is facilitated, passed on, and black belts are developed. Instructors are groomed, and refined, small and large training opportunities are presented; students are always the first priority.

Just a Few Words on the Organizational Spirit

The purpose of the organization cannot be to just promote that organization.

Even monolithic structures will eventually implode. They must be principle-driven and people-first. High ideals, goals, spirited training, respect for rules of conduct that have been handed down generation to generation, and tirelessly dedicated karate teachers define traditional karate. Karate was evolving from a great need for human survival before karate organizations ever entered the landscape.

Hundreds of years before karate organizations appeared, karate was developing out of the necessity for the human survival of unarmed people against armed and unarmed aggressors. In fact, as we know from the general history of the many karate styles evolving, the most serious karate development occurred in spite of, and even secretly from, political and military organizations and governments. If you research very old karate photos or films you see training on beaches, fields, back yards, or in small crowded gyms with people looking in, trying to mimic what they see going on because there is just no room. Conditions were bare minimum.

Many long term successful organizations have not been formed as high profit business models. Many of ours in the Central States Shotokan Karate are decades old and still going strong. Dozens of instructors have continued teaching and training around the country with an atmosphere that is rather community based; more family-type dojos, spread across communities in a wide variety of organizations, universities, and the like. If the need to maintain a profit-first based motives are primary, this may compromise instruction quality in order to "pay the bills." Of course, the reality of keeping the dojo doors open and the lights on is a cold, understandable reality. Word of mouth is probably always going to be the best

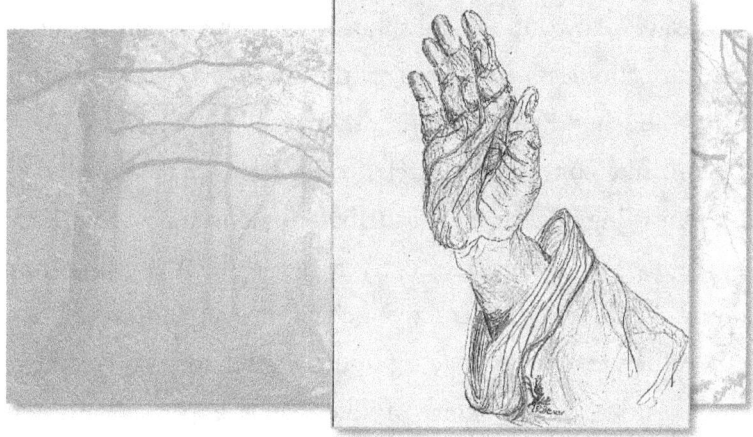

recruiting and retention method, so a student-centered environment with quality instruction is always crucial. If students know their karate development and well-being is utmost, then the rest will take care of itself.

Our main purpose has always been to simply study and teach quality karate. Organizational goals should allow students of all ages to study, practice and develop according to their varied abilities. Lifetime-learning of karate should be a primary motivation. We have tried to bring students along using the karate principles outlined by Funakoshi and his peers using international quality standards. If organizations use well-grounded karate training, excellent knowledgeable instruction, and student-centered goals, they become strong from the inside-outward, just like the students.

Organizations need people; people do not necessarily need organizations.

Finding Yourself: Looking Within for Answers

There are many unhappy, disillusioned people, feeling diffused and directionless, depressed with low self-esteem, abusing drugs, abusing themselves and other people. Sadly, they scurry around like confused squirrels from one thing to another to find meaning in their lives, usually looking in the wrong places by habit. Some continue to try to get different results from doing the same self-destructive behaviors over and over.

When I was in college, a popular expression was "trying to find yourself." It's kind of like being a peg, desperately searching for the square, round, or triangular hole to fit into. But that's difficult without knowing what shaped peg you are.

One supreme property of karate-do is the inherent introspection and self- discovery that is a basis of growth and improvement. Developing a clearer self-perception helps in discovering personal qualities that may be hidden. Self-image and esteem improve because of discoveries of previously untapped talents and wonderful human potentials. We learn more about ourselves. Clearer perceptions of reality and personal discovery of strengths and weaknesses are drawn from long-term training.

CHAPTER 28

Seeing Things as They Are -- Not as They Seem

Self-Delusion

STUDENTS WHO PUT THEIR EGO ASIDE remain inquisitive and sponge-like on all things karate, seriously listening to, and faithfully acting on their instructor's words. Many can eventually become superb instructors in their own right.

Students who do not put their ego aside, because they always know more than their teachers, or because it is easier to make excuses than to make changes, become nothing more.

Self-examination and self-change are very difficult. Grappling with them honestly is the way of budo, and a hallmark of karate training.

Prejudice: A Weakness to Eliminate

Having and cultivating blind prejudice (pre-judgement) demonstrates ignorance and often unnecessary stupidity in an inexcusable form. Tactically, it makes you vulnerable to serious mistakes from premature incorrect conclusions. Prejudices are dangerous to unjustified and innocent victims and equally to the person having them. On social levels prejudices are well known for baseless and destructive tribal behaviors.

Historically speaking, prejudice has resulted in racism, horrible and destructive atrocities, due to perceived differences in people, especially used to gain power and to manipulate others. Genocide, terrorism and social injustice are extreme results that take place in our world even today.

Well known historical examples are Hitler murdering millions, apartheid, tribal and religious genocides in Eastern Europe, Africa, in the Middle East and around the world, brutality against Native Americans, and the slavery and crimes against humanity, and the list goes on. All are a sad statement of weakness in humanity. But then the whole purpose of karate-do is to strengthen and combat weakness of all sorts. To fortify our own weaknesses and observe and take advantage of weaknesses in individual or multiple attackers.

Seemingly harmless, unknown prejudices, not easily recognized in ourselves can cause extremely self-destructive decisions. Prejudices are bad tactical dispositions. This is not the same as assessing the situation. These are pre-judgments in our brain software that can cause faulty assessments --- lack of clarity in sizing up danger. These cause errors in the judgement required to correctly size up a situation and assess the correct course of action.

Self-defense decisions need to be made flawlessly in milliseconds with life in the balance. Flawed judgement can be detrimental to your health. In karate our job is to see accurately how things ARE, not what they may SEEM. Learning to make correct decisions using good judgement is critical on idealist and practical levels.

Let's look at some potentially dangerous examples:

All salesmen seem to have your best interest at heart? Sure, they do. A friendly phone voice says you have won the Sweepstakes, so they need your social security number and please send them $500 just to hold it for you. That can't end well.

Or perhaps you visit a friend to see his brand new .45 automatic pistol and you assume that it was unloaded and harmless because, after all, it's on his coffee table. So you pick it up and look down the wrong end of the barrel without asking. What could go wrong with that? Not such good judgment.

Or, since you live in the suburbs, or in the countryside, you don't have to lock your doors even overnight while you snooze. You and your stuff and your family will be safe. This could get you robbed and dead. Sleep well. No worries.

Or maybe in a karate match, you assume all gray-haired guys with torn looking old belts are just old and slow. This might really get you some bruises and breaks.

Absolutely, assessments and judgment calls need to be made by sizing up situations ahead of time to determine a course of action. That is why we develop alertness and observational abilities to assess dangerous situations rapidly. In all martial arts objective observation and acute awareness skills are critical. Correct judgments are made by evaluating behaviors and actions, not by assumptions.

In training, if you want to test this out, simply face your opponent and decide ahead of time what he is going to do; like flipping a coin to baselessly pre-judge the attack and prepare just exactly for that guess. Go for it! Simple enough. Now according to your guess, get ready, and go! Success? Or Oops? Ouch? You decided that your opponent was going to kick but instead, a punch explodes in your face? The best posture is to assume nothing, pre-judge nothing, keep your eyes open and your mind clear, react to what actually comes, and not to think what might come. Assessment and adaptation to objective reality is paramount.

Tactical Food for Thought

Strategically and tactically, assumptions and incorrect judgments are weaknesses that provide openings for your opponent to use against you. The masters throughout history have stressed "living in the now." React and observe only what "is" helps success. Otherwise we are easily tricked, mislead, and set up by our opponent to be a victim. Prejudice is a weakness to be used by your opponent if they sense it.

One of my students, a young black belt, fought in a tournament. Looking across the ring at his opponent, he saw an aged, graying haired man wearing a faded black belt. But after all, this was the black belt division so he felt up to the task. The young Shodan saw across from him, an older, slower "appearing" guy, someone that should be an easy match for his youth and blinding speed. The referee said, *"Hajime!"*

Seconds later, a foot sweep and a punch ended the match, with my young warrior on the floor, dazed, and looking at the ceiling. *"Ippon!"* My student told me later that he should have known better. The "old guy" with the faded hair and belt had experience and wisdom as well.

CHAPTER 29

Responsibilities and Ethics: Teaching Deadly Force

THE LEGENDARY STAN SCHMIDT was the first non-Japanese to be on the Shihankai of the Japan Karate Association (JKA) in Japan. He was Chief Instructor of the South African JKA that published its own journal. He wrote several wonderful books describing in great detail how he felt karate persons should conduct themselves and shares many of his own trials and adventures.

He is an absolutely inspiring karate man in everything he does. He told me once that in his karate journey he had become friends worldwide with so many wonderful people, that he did not think of himself as from any one country but that he considered himself a "citizen of the world." He is a wonderful example of the idealism of karate bringing people together, transcending borderlines. He often recounts the first karate book he ever read that inspired his own life-time karate journey that said, "The karate man trains every day." This means much more than just doing a few techniques daily. It means incorporating karate into many aspects your daily life and having that "beginners mind," learning how approach the challenges that life throws at us to do just that.

Training the best karate-do spirit cannot be comprehensively addressed without a discussion of the *Dojo Kun* (Dojo Code). The Dojo Kun is a guideline for the correct spirit you must strive for. You might think of it as daily spirit training for correct conduct, the proper spirit of a productive human being. All karate training is a daily work in progress. We cannot reach perfection but we keep chopping our way through life's jungles the best we can.

I always actually had great fun in over three decades of teaching in public high schools incorporating karate into my daily work process. I could write another book on those stories but it is enough to say here that karate in my pocket every day was a necessity. I taught automotive collision repair classes and had a very popular program. It incorporated both class room learning and lab work (fixing cars in a pretty large shop area). In class I used karate for everything from breaking up fights, with 17-year-olds suddenly, and with no warning, launching themselves, desks and chairs at each other over God only knows what. I had to leap into action to prevent their mutual destruction, but I had to do so with the calm resolve to protect other students and let all know (at least think) I was in complete control of the situation. I give karate training the credit for helping me stay calm in the face of the explosion of violence and teenage hormones, be able to assess the situation, adapt and react immediately and appropriately to bring peace, harmony and order back to my classroom.

To teach the labs, my students would drive ten cars every hour into my lab (nerves of steel required for me directing this process) and then I would scurry around teaching and mentoring their work. I always joked that this was like any other class but I gave them weapons: torches, grinders, hammers, and the like. I was surrounded by noise and movement every second. I had to be alert for accidents, students making poor and dangerous choices, and to see dangerous hazards before "mishaps" could occur. We painted the vehicles after the students repaired the body parts, so we always had paints and thinners under the same roof with sparks form welders and grinders. At any moment, if the two mixed, it would have been an explosion and ball of fire that few if any of us would have survived. I literally practiced global awareness every second. My daily karate mental attitudes paid off and over a thousand students would graduate with job skills and I'm alive to write this.

In one instance I had been on alert for a gang intimidation issue and was bound and determined not to let them act out under my watch. A boy came up to me and shared that three students were planning to jump him during my lab class. I told him to give me a heads up then stand behind me and he would be okay. I was alert but did little preplanning, having no idea how or when the mayhem might materialize. I was aware for signs of trouble and I think my confident posture and my visible attentiveness were signal enough that trouble did not develop. I later that day received a grateful call from his parents and counselors: reward enough. Every day would be another new day. A few years later a blue uniformed, fully armed police officer, dropped in to visit me unannounced. I was thinking, "Oh good I forgot to renew my car sticker!" But it was the student that had come to me during class, that I had told to stand behind me and he would be okay. He was there purposely to thank me again.

I used my karate learned behaviors every day at my job to protect myself, be a better teacher, and guard the welfare of my students. I had even had reworded karate dojo code of conduct

rules and posted them in my classroom as rules and my expectations for all to follow; to get along together and make the best productive and safe learning environment for us all.

In daily life, as a true martial artist, we must attempt to be a productive human who, constantly working to be better. Karate is a lifetime learning process. All of the mental skills we use along with technique are really very helpful if practiced. Admittedly, the scope of this book has only scratched the surface of true fighting spirit creation and use. My words fall short of descriptions and solutions that can be realized with diligent daily effort. But that's what the dojo is for. Luckily, like anything, the results become good habits that over time become second nature. That's when the feelings of mental and physical karate training are absorbed and calm strength and confidence materialize.

Almost every credible karate style utilizes some kind of code of conduct. In Shotokan we have our own from Funakoshi in the form of his *20 Precepts* and his five Dojo Kun. These have been outlined and used in Shotokan since its beginning.

A wonderful quote attributed to the sword saint, Miyamoto Musashi, is to "do nothing that is of no use." If you accept the mantle of "karate student," then you must accept the proper spirit of behaviors and conduct outlined in the Dojo Kun. Self-improvement is the "everyday karate spirit," and must be considered in rank exams as a prominent part of the evaluation along with fighting spirit and technical ability. Of all karate skill sets, the everyday karate spirit and attitudes practiced in and out of the dojo should be an important part of rank advancement. It's obviously a must with youth but is important for adults as well.

Remember the statement that inspired Sensei Stan Schmidt from the first karate book he ever read was, "The karate man trains every day." We may not punch and kick every day, but we can certainly practice the everyday karate-do spirit.

So far, our emphasis has been on exploring ways to enhance and magnify the spirit for combat training to develop all of those intangibles to use in life-threatening situations. We can look at (and teach students to look at) the Dojo Kun as our everyday training to conduct ourselves and to strive to be a little better each day than the day before. As with all things in karate-do, it is maintaining the process that is most important. It is a personal journey.

The Dojo Kun may look like an innocuous little list to memorize. Far from it, it is a code of conduct used to temper even the fiercest karate fighter to develop into an extremely high quality human being. Character must be just as good and strong as technique.

Dojo Ethics Teaching Deadly Force

President Theodore Roosevelt said, "Speak softly and carry a big stick." Now examine the "speaking softly" part of karate. We do not give out a driver's license to anyone who has not learned the rules of the road and shown they have minimum safety skills. We do not give gun-carrying permits and hunting licenses without proof of safety instruction. Both of these give people deadly force in their hand, and we considered ethics and proper safety skills to be necessary. Karate is learning to develop deadly force. This requires character instruction, ethics instruction, and high standards of personal conduct.

Chapter 30

Funakoshi's Dojo Kun: A Closer Look

First, my intention here, as with every other explanation in this book, is absolutely not to preach. I am only sharing ideas and thoughts to be helpful.

I we can drum into students that the "mind is as important to train as the body" in karate, we set a premise for all the rest that follows. If students can understand why "karate must begin and end with courtesy" and that "there is no first attack in karate," then they are off to a good start assimilating their most hard-core karate training into their lives to become great productive citizens.

Long ago in Japan, as Funakoshi worked to introduce karate into Japanese society, he needed karate presented in the best light possible as it was introduced into the "highbrow" academic world of Japanese universities. As a life-long karate student, I am still learning grappling with processing and incorporating "karate spirit training" and unlimited other karate aspects into my own attitudes and behaviors: life is short, and I'll never get it done, so it's always a challenge and work in process. It's that journey thing again. But like that tiny plant fighting up through concrete, we can never give up. Humbly, my goal is to offer explanations and suggestions that are simplified so that karate students of all levels can take something to benefit from. Any time I use the pronoun "you," I really mean you and I and everyone that might benefit. My attempt here is to merely offer some ideas and interpretations for instructors to use with their own students.

Let's take a closer look at the *Dojo Kun* (Dojo Codes) I've been using these with students and for myself for decades. Students receive and understand them very well. They actually enjoy talking about them and shouting them out during classes. Mental and physical karate training is a package deal. We try to address both in every class.

"Hitotsu, jinkaku kansei ni tsutomeru koto!"

Always strive to perfect your character

Simply put; this is a process of each day, trying to be a better person each day than the day before. For children, we can discuss this easily in terms of being a "good citizen," working hard in school, and treating others, young and old, fairly and, politely, etc. Teach them never to bully others, and to be a brave advocate of being kind and strong when they see others being bullied. Taking questions from this age group for discussions is always interesting!

For adults, life can become more extremely complicated, but at least adults already have a grasp on the meaning of the words, "strive for perfecting character." Before getting discouraged, understand that this describes a work always in progress. But at least all karate stresses goals to strive for. For adults, life challenges can be overwhelming, but the positive influences of karate, church, family, friends, and even community service organizations can offer hope. Karate instructors have no control over other aspects but can insure that dojo life is supportive and saturated with positive character-building energy.

Little by little we build on how we conduct ourselves today and try to improve the content our character tomorrow. This particular *dojo kun* is rather all-encompassing; it can cover alot. It is a challenge to reflect and try to improve ourselves, just as we would train consistently to better our karate techniques. And just as our technique is constantly being learned, maintained, and polished, our character will always be a work in progress as well. Trying to perfect something that can never be perfected just comes with the karate-do territory.

"*Hitotsu, makoto no michi o mamoru koto!*"
Following a path of sincerity, and honesty

This everyday spirit challenge is a directive to be truthful, sincere, and honest. Like striving for perfection of character in our first dojo kun, this is a daily work in progress. We must, in our dealings with other people and ourselves, try to shape our character into one of integrity and credibility. The "path" or "*michi*" illustration is important. If you walk through tall grass once, you may see your trail. If you are honest and sincere, even against your own selfish desires once, then it may be easier the next time. The more you walk the tall grass each day, the easier your correct path is to see, even until eventually the soft trail is now a dirt path; unmistakably clear out in front. The more sincerity and honesty is consciously practiced, the easier it is to make even the difficult correct choices. This earns the respect of others. As a work in progress, new challenges will come. As long as we are principle driven working on sincerity and honesty earn the respect of others. Good sincere and honest choices will become easier; the path ahead will have more clarity. Karate principles are simple in writing but for all of us as karate students, the devil is in the daily skirmishes. In the political environment that involves even our national leaders, lying and corruption seem to be the norm. There are many good and bad examples to turn into teaching moments for our young people. Following the road of honesty and sincerity is a choice that enthusiastic karate students are eager to tackle.

"Hitotsu, doryoku no seishin o yashinau koto!"

Be enthusiastic --- foster the spirit of effort

Fostering the spirit of enthusiasm and effort simply means that you should wake up each day, take a deep breath, and give it your best shot. Too many people succeed at making themselves, and everyone they meet, miserable. Be enthusiastic and keep a positive outlook. In an enthusiastic state of mind, you will feel better, and you will surround yourself in and out of your dojo with other enthusiastic people. Enthusiasm is contagious and highly productive. By purposely working on enthusiasm each day, it will become another rewarding path that is easier to walk. Expect enthusiasm to be highly visible in the dojo. Expect your instructor, in his or her own way, to stress its importance in karate and self-defense, and its importance each day of your life. If you are an instructor reading this, then you know the drill.

"Hitotsu, reigi o omonzuru koto!"
Be polite, respectful, and courteous

Once I saw an advertisement at Sensei Randall Hassell's dojo in St. Louis that he was even using in newspaper ads. I wrote it down and immediately posted it on my classroom bulletin board in my high school classroom, and I still quote it often when teaching my karate classes. All right, it may be a little corny, but many people entering the dojo don't understand the idea of being taught to punch and kick people, and in the next moment we are telling them they must be humble, polite, and courteous to others. The quote goes simply like this: "In karate, we punch and kick politely."

Why is courtesy an important concept to karate students? Well, for one Funakoshi, one of the founders of our modern-day karate-do, said so. It all relates to perfecting character and incorporating karate-do and budo into your everyday lifestyle. Karate is all about strengthening the student with a high level of physical skill sets, high levels of mental skills and positive, outstanding character traits.

This Dojo Kun fosters strong feedback that makes it fascinating. The more courteous and respectful you are in and out of the dojo, the more people will reciprocate similar behaviors back. In fact, you should see a recurring pattern to this and the other standards of conduct. It's easier to act with these positive traits in the dojo because your sempai can whip you into shape if you don't. But practicing in the dojo is an important introduction to how we should conduct ourselves in a courteous manner outside of the dojo. You bring honor, admiration, and respect to yourself and to karate. Respect others and display and adhere to principles of proper etiquette. We must be the gentle warrior. Students learn that being polite is a position of strength.

"Hitotsu, kekki no yu o imashimuru koto"

Refrain from impetuous and violent behavior

This Dojo Kun is a double-edged sword. Often you will see it in a simplified form as, "Control bad temper." Remember that when Funakoshi Sensei introduced his Shotokan to the wider world, he didn't want karate to be misunderstood as just a violent activity with no redeeming values. He had come from an education vocation as his day-job, responsible for the education and character development of the school children he worked with. And in Japan, he needed karate presented in the best light possible as it was introduced into the academic world of Japanese universities. Therefore, karate students losing their temper and reflecting badly on karate at a time when it needed outstanding credibility was important.

This last *Dojo Kun* could have just as easily been the first listed. I have taught karate in high schools and colleges since the early 1970s. In an educational environment, especially with younger people, the administration and the parents are usually

happy with the high-spirited, rough and tumble sports like soccer, football, wrestling, and the like. However, even now, Hollywood and video games set the stage for misunderstandings about what we know is a beautiful martial art. Having college kids, for example, learning to punch and kick "politely," and then go out to fraternity parties or bars and create mayhem is a huge, counter-productive disaster. That kind of impetuous and violent behavior is insulting and truly disgusting. It destroys the credibility of karate clubs and instructors. Trouble and needlessly distasteful behavior reflects poorly on karate, and like a stone splashing into a still pond, there are ripples radiating outward on all sides.

Now let's consider the flipside. As usual, in all things karate, there is more than meets the eye here. Having a bad temper and starting karate means that at least you are now getting instructions on controlling it. Osamu Ozawa once said that, "All violence is bad." This doesn't mean that violent measures used to counter violent attacks are not necessary. Surviving an attack by using the most powerful high-spirited response may be needed. But you must remember that, like using a firearm for self-defense, behind every bullet released and every punch that connects to its target, there may be a lawyer or prosecutor waiting to ask hard questions. These types of questions are much easier answered from a standpoint that you are known to be a calm and sensible person who only uses deadly force when it's a last resort.

Students who have an uncontrollable temper, will be "counseled" in the dojo or may need to be expelled from the dojo, which must be a controlled environment. Out on the street, your bad temper will pop up at unpredictable times and cause very dangerous problems. You'd be the road-rage person, or the bar bum. Remember the old saying, "Never take a knife-hand to a gun fight" (original phrase altered by the author). If you are not already wrecking your own personal relationships and your life in general, sooner or later you may run into someone who is tougher than you with an unpredictable temper just as bad as your own.

Impetuous behavior can kill the smartest fox. (This goes well with my discussions on prejudice as well.) I like to refer to this as the "bull in the china shop syndrome." Impetuous behavior is impulsive and sometimes jumping to premature conclusions that prove wrong, and if punctuated with violence can result in disaster. Guarding against it is kind of like saying "Look before you leap in a mine field." It is much better to study situations and think of other better choices to make, if at all possible. Jumping to conclusions without thinking is usually the most impetuous, most dangerous, and most self-destructive way for you to proceed. Guard against impetuous behavior for your own benefit and encourage others to follow your lead.

Reflections

Karate is a principle driven endeavor in both mental and physical realms. It is karate-do: always a work in progress and seldom easy. But that's why the smallest bit of progress is so rewarding. Just as we train to ward off a physical attack with a clear mind, we have to train the spirit for warding off psychological and verbal attacks and confrontations. One important advantage to the skills resulting from serious study of the *Dojo Kun* is the ability to mentally and emotionally face the stressful challenges of today's life demands. Integrity and calm determination amid today's hectic pace is a calm strength. Be the calm eye of the hurricane.

The karate spirit is one of balancing the enthusiastic fighting spirit and a confident, calm, patient, and honorable spirit. We must always strive for this.

Chapter 31

Osamu Ozawa: A Samurai Story

OUR EXPERIENCES WITH MASTER OSAMU OZAWA were far too brief. But the things we learned and the impression he made upon my own karate spirit training were extreme. He was, after all, a direct student of Master Gichin Funakoshi. If you can locate an old copy of his biography, *Samurai Journey*, written by Randall Hassell, it's a very thought-provoking read. Hassell spent several years of long and painstaking personal interviews to write it. Sometimes Shihan Ozawa would share heart-felt personal drama about himself and other top leaders of his day, his own sempai and friends in Japan, when karate was growing, and beginning to evolve and reach out world-wide. He had some very unique stories from friendships to squabbles, and only to tell Sensei Hassell to delete those, edit them out, because he did not want to offend anyone. I was charmed to hear a few that I certainly will not reveal.

On another excursion, I couldn't resist asking him about what I read about Korean Tae-Kwon Do masters that had trained with Gichin Funakoshi in Japan. "Why yes!" He said. "I knew them!" He proceeded to rattle off details, names, experiences, and the like; as I began busily weaving through traffic to get him to our next class on time and in one piece. It was an incredible history lesson.

My acquaintance with Ozawa Sensei was during clinics that Carl Hartter and I hosted in our Central Illinois Shotokan dojos, and our national ASKA events at Randall Hassell's dojos in St. Louis, as well as our visits to Master Ozawa's tournament and clinics in Las Vegas. The most fun and candid moments were driving him around, long conversational dinners, visits in hotel rooms watching CNN, and once even sitting on a curb of a busy street. If you knew him, you can hear Ozawa's voice as you read his biography, as if he were with you in the room. If he was happy he was cheerful and magnetic, if he wasn't happy, well, you quickly understood that too.

I witnessed Ozawa's strong traditional karate spirit quickly! He was clearly a modern-day samurai. Yes, he could be as fierce as he needed, with the yakuza blade scars he showed us on his arms to prove it. But the more you got to know him, the more you could appreciate his multifaceted character, his optimism, his limitless energy and creativity, and his love for karate. He was lean in stature and a very considerate, humble, giant of a personality.

He once called my home at 2 a.m., accidentally. He said his son had suddenly taken ill, he had to fly to Japan to see him, and he was clearly very upset. I had no idea how he even had my home phone, but he was trying to reach Randall Hassell to postpone a book interview for an emergency trip to Japan. He spilled out his problem and I quickly fumbled to find Sensei Hassell's number and gave it to him. He apologized over and over for bothering me. Granted, I was in a surprised stupor as I tried to clear my head, and fumble for phone numbers, to be of assistance. He was so upset, I felt sorry for him, and I was happy I could help.

Another example: we had flown him in for a weekend of clinics and I had painted him an oil painting of Mount Fuji in Japan. After class, I presented it to him in front of our students. I was astonished to see that not only was he appreciative, but his eyes welled up with a tear. He was so happy. He pointed to a spot on the painting and said, "My mother once lived right about here."

Make no mistake, he was a motivational taskmaster in class; telling stories of his own training years, chewing someone out one minute, and cracking jokes the next.

He commanded respect without saying a word. You see, when it came to the karate spirit, Osamu Ozawa was a master example of someone conquering seemingly insurmountable obstacles. I feel fortunate that my students and I were able to hear his astonishing story in his own words. He was the real deal. A modern samurai and in a frightening traditional sense. Near the end of WWII, he was trained to fly planes and assigned the dubious honor of being a kamikaze pilot.

As a matter of fact, Ozawa and my own father were in the Pacific islands at the exact same time, but of course on opposite sides. My father had joined for the duration of the war in the United States Navy. He was a 17- year-old sailor stationed on a troop carrier where he was an antiaircraft machine gunner. I have a wonderful old photo of his ship with the station on board where he manned his antiaircraft gun. He said that he and his friends often worried about their ship being hit by kamikaze pilots and submarines. Once, a Japanese submarine surfaced near his ship, pulled up close, and then finally right alongside. Dad said he thought he was a goner! But thankfully, the sub was only there to surrender. I am so happy that my father and Master Ozawa didn't come near each other in the Pacific.

At the very end of the war, Ozawa said he and other teenage boys were the last of the (kamikaze) pilots, waiting their turn to go on their final mission. "Most planes," he said, "were in horrible mechanical condition at the very end of the war, (like his would be), and often crashed on take-off. We just watched them, waiting for our day to be called up." As fate would have it, his own plane flipped upside down and crashed on take-off, leaving him helpless in the hospital for weeks afterward until the war ended.

Remarkably, Ozawa survived WWII in post-war Japan, was a millionaire and a pauper several times, helped Funakoshi introduce karate to the West, was a TV director, and a proud citizen of Las Vegas. At the time of his passing, Ozawa was the most senior Japanese karate instructor (in terms of time and age) in the Western Hemisphere.

More Than Just a Letter

Once, as we put him on his plane for home in Las Vegas, I gave him a couple of magazine articles that I had written about karate-do. I soon received a very gracious "thank you" letter from him. It contained, surprisingly, an eerie lesson, as you will soon see. In his letter he said:

Dear Rick,

Thank you very much for your wonderful articles. American karate must be taken care of by American(s) who know what will be (of) benefit for millions of Americans. Our generation almost finishing. I hope we can get together...

Sincerely,

Osamu Ozawa

If we look at his unique letter closely, he kind of lays out what he feels our duty as Americans in karate is and is straight to the point. He seems to be passing the flame on to new generations of American karate students.

He says simply, but profoundly I think, that Americans know what is best for the future of American Karate, and that the future of karate that future is now in our hands.

And then he closes with the rather cryptic, thought provoking admission.

Master Osamu Ozawa closed my letter with:

"Our generation almost finishing."

Ozawa Sensei passed this challenge on to all of us. Keep in mind that Ozawa was one of the handful of original Japanese who brought Karate to the West. He was saying that his generation of masters, that brought us karate, was nearly finished. The quality of American karate is now up to us.

CHAPTER 32

The Power of Commitment

*"Karate is like boiling water;
without continuous heat, it soon becomes cold."*

--- GICHIN FUNAKOSHI

IN GENERAL, LACK OF COMMITMENT sets up repeated failures in all aspects of life. Without it, we see others succeed at making themselves miserable, not accomplishing many, many things that are well within their abilities and intelligence. Sadly, they fall short of their best efforts. And they will know it.

For right NOW, in terms of karate-do and other martial arts, lack of purpose and conviction lowers training expectations and acquired skills. Approaching training halfheartedly, and results will be lackluster. Habitual hesitation in fighting or kumite will cause frustrating failures and grief (not to mention bruises, injuries, and other losses). The original masters who formulated the crucial components of martial art training did so from trial and error in actual survival situations. Commitment to accumulated practice is one of those "magic ingredients" and we must study and respect their judgement.

Spirit training combines wide variety of physiological and psychological forms we can use in and out of karate contexts.

One example that is well-known, is the high-spirited adrenal surge that causes little old ladies to lift cars to save a grandchild. And of course, karate performers slamming through boards and blocks that are harder than their own flesh and bones.

Most significant here is the visible, controlled outburst of the karate spirit, in the form of the ear-bursting *kiai!* accompanying karate technique, coming from someone who only seconds before was of the calm, clear-minded, mild-mannered person contributing to the good of the community.

The correct karate disposition is of the calm and clear-minded person, outlined in Funakoshi's *Dojo Kun* and his *20 Precepts,* who if necessary can tap into the energized fighting spirit appropriate to overcome adversities. The karate easily seen by the average person is the tip of the iceberg. Karate-do training is the not obvious two thirds of the iceberg pushing up from underneath.

Spirited karate training boosts essential energy reserves while we can be calm and confident, with that acquired explosiveness on tap. Combining spirit training and technical karate training is ideal. When you combine technique with superior mental skills and an indomitable spirit, you become a force to be reckoned with.

With commitment to long and short-term goals all these potentials can be put to good use. You have more control over your destiny.

There have been few one-word traits that have accomplished as much in the history of mankind as "commitment." We have notably used commitment to accomplish tasks individually or for populations acting in unison toward goals. We have crossed oceans to find new worlds. We have built cures for diseases to save humanity. We have built nuclear bombs to destroy humanity. With proper commitment, perhaps we will save our world from climate change, starvation, and needless genocides and war. One day, in 1896 a couple of bicycle mechanics built a glider, and less than 70 years later we landed on the moon. The spirit of commitment is a constructive trait for us all to respect, to cultivate, and to use.

Like the other energizing human traits that we nurture and activate into use as a direct product of karate training, the "Spirit of Commitment" has very real immediate uses for us. It is through devoted, regular, and disciplined training that we see what can be possible by putting our nose to the metaphorical grindstone. Commitment is one of those powerful karate reinforced character traits that facilitate good changes in lives forever.

I have a plaque on the wall of my dojo with these words inscribed on it and I see it every day. "Karate is like boiling water: if not given continuous heat, It soon becomes cold." This inscription on the wall of my dojo seems nice, clever, and at first glance, relatively benign. To say the least, it has its own resonance of power, almost haunting, forever undaunted in challenging me to keep training. The analogy is self-explanatory because this is karate-do. The need for empty-hand fighting and survival is probably in our DNA, as all survival has been. As far back as a time when Samurai were settling all sorts of issues right or wrong, diplomatic and political differences, and all out wars, with swords, knives, and eventually guns, the unfortunate option of having to fight to the death stripped of weapons was always a possibility. Stopping was not an option.

Far more crucial than the long traditions of fighting with weapons, even before it had a name, the commitment to training in empty-hand fighting for pure survival was innate and paramount.

Commitment Training

One cannot learn karate for a while, and totally stop training for long periods, and expect hard-earned karate skill sets to remain indefinitely. In fact, they will too soon become a pleasant, but distant memory.

I try to encourage students who have taken time off, months, years, and so on, by telling them that they will be surprised how quickly they will remember what they've forgotten. However, I must give them a reality check if they were 16 years old when they first trained, and now they are 36, by explaining that they will not heal as fast trying to regain their skill. Soreness will be a constant companion at first. If they are now 46 years old, they need to go slower to recover but that the benefits far outweigh not training. If they are 56 or more, the values of extending ranges of motion and general fitness along with defensive victim-proofing, are more important as ever; even potentially life-saving!

That said there is much research into muscle memory to suggest that after considerable training, the muscles and tissues of the body "remember" what they "knew" and come back more quickly with renewed training. I've had many people who trained in high school and as life got more complicated afterward, they dropped out of karate, only to come back to me 20 years later. As adults they are more stable and mature, realizing that commitment leads to more fulfillment. Many are very seasoned strong black belts now.

So, I often encouragingly say, "It's just like riding a bicycle; once you learn, you never forget." (We've all heard that expression.) I forget to mention, however, that you may have ridden a bicycle from the time you were three years old until you were in college. Another anomaly that I try not to mention, is that our clock does not "reset" back to our previous stating point. Watch out! You are not now exactly who you were, and your brain may make bills your body can't pay. This is certainly an example of the "tortoise beating the hare." Go slow at first, in order to go faster later. Be committed and patient.

I read some encouraging news about marathon runners, Olympic athletes, and the like. The experts said that it takes just as long to get out of good condition as it did to get into that condition. Studies show that athletes who commit to high standards of continuous training, get injured, and take time off in rehab, can begin training soon, and they quickly regain their conditioning. In fact, in short rehab situations or illness, the rest of the body gets rested and performs at higher levels sometimes than before.

It does not really apply to someone who trains at karate, takes a few years off, and then comes back expecting Father Time to leave everything intact, just like before. Sorry. So, what's the good news, you ask? If we can adhere to Funakoshi's axioms of being committed to incorporating, even if only a little at first, long term accumulative karate training, we can regain much.

It should be continually stressed; how important it is to incorporate karate-do into our lifestyle. Training even a little bit, as jobs and families allow is beneficial. Karate was made to help us all.

If you get injured, follow your doctor's orders, go to therapy, and explain that you train at karate and it's important to your health, fitness, self-esteem, stress management, and so forth. They will be happy to assist you with what to do and what not to do.

Commitment to a thing that benefits your life short-term (defending against attack) and long-term (physical and psychological health and wellbeing), is not just admirable. It is an important and a self-empowering life skill.

People often are in awe observing a skilled karate student performing a good basic kata. They often stare witnessing the human karate work of art. The same people jump with glee when their favorite baseball player hits a home run, or a football player runs in a touchdown, or the NBA player makes a half-court basket. The great mystery of seemingly superhuman feats of all sorts are hidden in plain sight. Even just average people can perform exceptionally well if they study a thing persistently. Most people, however, cannot comprehend studying any one thing continually to reach some exceptional level toward its perfection.

Funakoshi said, *"The effects of karate are cumulative."*

If you can only train a few minutes a day, that's fine. Even if you are laid up in a hospital (as I have found from my own unpleasant experiences) mentally visualizing karate is a great uplifting feeling of freedom! Sparring tactics are fun to visualize, and you can always win. Besides, visualization of doing techniques is a powerful procedure that Olympians and professional athletes in other arenas use, so it's bound to help you and me. And the most crucial, common, redeeming behavioral component to conquering problems and challenges in karate, and just life in general: "commitment." Don't be surprised if, as you watch many people around you set themselves up for failure, you see that a lack of commitment is often a huge factor.

The benefits of consistent karate training are well-known and legendary. Any good instructor tries to draw the connections of the dojo lesson to multiple aspects of life outside of the dojo. Karate focuses attention on those positive character strengths that cause success and stimulate growth. No one said karate would be easy. That's exactly the reason we become stronger and more productive. Attitudes that we learn inside the dojo are directly applicable outside.

Commitment: *energy is given powerfully to a goal while ignoring doubts and trepidations and persistently never giving up.*

Chapter 33

Persevere!

PERSEVERE! If you have studied Tsun Tzu's *Art of War*, or Musashi's *Go Rin No Sho*, you know that the most important tactics and strategies can be applied to small scale skirmishes with individuals and to large-scale wars with armies. The spirit of perseverance and commitment factor heavily into these.

Perseverance can be decisive in the outcome of one on one combat and competitions, military confrontations, team competitions including karate and all sorts of sports and human activities. Through healthy perseverance and underhanded covert activity, the ongoing policies of countries (Ever hear of the Cold War?), and of ethnic, religious, political, terrorist, and activist groups are promoted and realized around the world.

Before 9/11 we didn't pay much attention to what we thought were "unofficial" terrorist groups who were feverishly committed to their own cowardly, demented causes. Our world is a multilayered sphere of unlimited interests, points of view, covert and overt actions, and fluid boundaries of millions of people committed to both compatible and competing agendas. "See things as they are, not as they seem."

On the good side with the good guys winning, vast ramifications of the long-term perseverance and dedication are quite amazing. From countries and armies, to you and I training, this spirit is huge and affects many things. If you have difficulties in your own spirit training in other topics we've studied in this book, and you have a firm grip on the spirit to persevere onward, then you will be able to overcome many obstacles with winning persistence.

I spoke of good and unnerving worldwide aspects of commitment and determination to give a healthy respect these character traits. They are valuable and useful in karate-do for many good reasons. The history of the world is saturated with instances of the most committed, often the underdog, overcoming seemingly impossible challenges.

Who was most committed to winning the war for our tiny original thirteen colonies? The British with their flashy, very attractive red coats, or the future Americans carving existences out of the wilderness?

Remember a teacher named Helen Keller? She graduated from college with high honors, wrote books and short stories and taught. She was committed to learning and using all her potential. Blind and deaf, she was committed to making the best use of the highest potential she had, against all odds.

For decades the Russian Bear ruled hockey in the Olympics without mercy until the 1980s, when a young USA Hockey team did the unthinkable and beat the bear for the Olympic Gold in hockey.

The greatest surprises from high-spirited commitment and rabid determination may be from not knowing you that you aren't supposed to succeed!

Back in my early days as an instructor, I admit to juggling the responsibilities of my day job, teaching, and running the karate club. The highest ranks in our new club were three brown belts when a regional tournament came up. Even as a

new karate club, we still trained four or five nights a week, all year-long. "There is no karate season," we would often brag to other student athletes and coaches. "Karate training is forever."

I told my "crack kumite team" of high school juniors that they would be competing against some of the best black and brown belts around Central Illinois.

"Don't worry about that," I said. "Just remember, always do your best, to do your best, and never, ever give up!" This became our karate dojo anthem.

"The secret is to be determined, persevere, train, and train, and train some more!" But honestly, I really thought we didn't have a prayer. This was their first tournament. I felt that they were dedicated. They all trained daily at the dojo and weekends on their own. I kept saying, "If you do your best, be very determined, commit to giving your best effort, then no matter the outcome, you can look at yourselves in the mirror and be proud!"

When the dust settled in the advanced kumite division in that tournament, my three underdog brown belts had won first, second, and third place! I was surprised and learned an important lesson myself. We were not very concerned about the outcome. I caused them to commit to bringing the best effort from every fiber in their bodies, and to never give up on themselves.

Here are some thoughts that really work. Training in the spirit of commitment and perseverance is like the story of the "Tortoise and the Hare." Be the hare, and you will go fast and furious, and then give up; and fail flatly. Be the tortoise: train every day, even for just a little bit. Stay committed, and slowly but surely, become strong and determined to press forward, to meet any challenge life offers you. Move forward even if it is just a little at a time. You will win; the hare will lose.

"If You Are Not Moving Forward, You Are Moving Backwards; Nothing Stays The Same."

Chapter 34

You Have the Power!

STAN SCHMIDT TOLD A WONDERFUL STORY about training on an air liner. He was on route to teach a clinic in St, Louis and to work with Randall Hassell on one of his books. On his plane from South Africa, about a 16-hour flight, as I recall he did kata! The catch was, this was his shortly after his car crash and his double hip replacement. (This is particularly inspirational for those of us with joint replacements.) He said that his body stiffened up, especially his hips. So, he went back to the airliner restroom and in the restroom, he did *Tekki* kata in as wide of a stance as his hips and the restroom size allowed; not very wide of course. But it allowed him to stretch and work off some steam. After sharing his story, he had us all do Tekki katas standing in a narrow straddle leg *Kiba-dachi,* pretend we were in an airplane restroom, and do the katas with no leg movement whatsoever. It worked. But I must say, it took thought on the first try. Later, when I had my own hip replacements, I remembered this lesson! When leaving the dojo, the support of instructors and peers is left behind, but we take our karate-do with us wherever we go.

After each karate training class when we leave the dojo, we are under our own power. When first starting out, or after a lay off for whatever reason, we must bring ourselves back into class to keep going. It's easy to quit. Gym memberships everywhere spike with New Year's resolutions, and then drop like a rock a few weeks later. Similar trends are in karate. That's why if the holistic view of karate-do is shown to be more relevant to benefit many facets of our everyday life, retention will stay at a much higher level. It makes more sense to do something during the week that might literally save your life on the weekend. It makes sense to so something a few times a week that makes you feel better and be healthier long term. I went to the doctor once for a routine physical and asked how I was doing? He said all blood chemistry and vital signs were great so whatever I was doing, keep doing it. Karate teaching and training 4 or 5 times a week was my answer, so it worked for me!

There are certainly reasons that you must stop or take a pause in going to class. The karate student can look to his or her karate as a source of strength to be used in other aspects of life, especially the ones that require fortitude. If we can't go to class, we just do what we can at home.

Some people like to try a thing for a short time, then move onto something else for a short time, but never find anything that holds much interest (especially if it requires work or resolve). They are easily bored, easily distracted. They typically short-change themselves. If you have a few karate lessons under your belt and this relates to you, you should probably quit karate now, and go try underwater basket weaving. I digress.

Karate becomes even more important with time and study as more benefits become enjoyable. Good karate takes longer to learn. After all, it is something that is highly relevant to survival, with beauty and power, and that has been evolving for hundreds of years.

It is the incorporation of karate into your lifestyle that is immediately and continuously rewarding. You are surrounding yourself with other ambitious people who soon become your peers, friends (and true friends), your mentors and instructors, almost like a new extended family. The sum of karate experiences incredibly boosts your self-esteem.

There will be those times when, as life goes on you may not be able to make it to the dojo for a time. Never fear! You won't have to quit karate. In fact, I have always tried to encourage my students to build kind of a parallel training plan to supplement what they might be doing in the dojo. This empowers them to "take their karate with them" when they leave the dojo. It's kind of a "Plan B."

Train in your apartment, home, yard!

I always encourage students to create a workout place in their home, apartment, garage or in their front yard (though the back yard will scare fewer neighbors). The neighbors will soon get used to the new karate person down the street. They may even think that the new normal is to do karate in the yard. And don't be surprised if you gain students to recruit or tutor from your own neighbors and friends.

The Never-Quitting Spirit

What we need to do is wave off and block some ordinary situations that some people may feel are karate-ending circumstances. By reading this, you are on the road to being more empowered. But things happen. That is just life. Remember that the more continuous karate training, the more confidence and bravery can be acquired to get past life's curve balls. And with a solid foundation in karate spirit training, you have positive attitudes and the optimism to turn the boulders thrown your way into gravel under your feet.

Think about karate training, challenging activities you survived, and the axioms of karate-do you are studying in class. Review them in your mind while you are at home, work and play.

The next time you train in the dojo, when you are doing warm ups, look up. As you and the other students are doing basics across the floor, again glance up. See anything? Are there any puppet strings? There were no puppet strings with a magical sensei pulling magic ropes to make you do karate. Sound bizarre? Here's the point: If you were hooked up like a puppet, and a sensei was holding the strings, dropped all the strings, and sent you home, you would be helpless --- void of karate benefits to take home.

But that is not the case --- you are not a puppet. You are trained to take all of your karate skills with you, to use whenever you need them --- out of the dojo and into your life.

You can take a person away from training, but karate training is not taken out of the person. This proves that you will have your karate skills with you even when a layoff occurs; when sick, starting a new job, going back to school, tending to an injury, getting a new girl- or boy-friend, when the car breaks down, and the list goes on and on. Karate skills are retained for quite some time.

All the masters throughout history had life changes. Every black belt I ever met had important challenges, life changes, illnesses, family problems, job and military obligations. We all have these, but it is how we work our way through these things that defines our character as human beings. Karate just helps give you that little extra empowerment that makes the speed bumps of life smaller.

Karate, seriously studied, provides strength of character, confidence, self-esteem, and the "steel" to weather your difficulties.

What would be the logic of giving up such a valuable commodity as karate training, that can keep us mentally sharp, optimistic and more physically energetic, to face the challenges that are guaranteed to come? Resist quitting the very thing that can give you incredible personal empowerment. If something takes away from training for a while, make up your mind ahead of time to continue a small bit of training as best you can. Use the "opportunity" to read more about all martial arts and seek out inspiration. Talk to others during your day who may also be training. It's amazing how many people are in a similar situation as you.

The important thing to understand is the self-empowered resource that karate-do brings to all who train.

You have the power!

CHAPTER 35

William J. Dometrich:
Quitting at New Thresholds

BACK IN THE EARLY 1970S, there was a collegiate tournament at Illinois State University, hosted by Sensei John Donahue and Sensei Shojiro Sugiyama was the Senior Japanese JKA Instructor in the Midwest, the Chief Arbitrator, and he had brought his own excellent team from his Chicago dojos.

Sensei William J. Dometrich, who has long since founded the United States Chito-ryu Karate Federation, and has written his wonderful biography, *The Endless Quest,* brought a very strong team of skilled blackbelts from Kentucky. A seemingly insignificant incident happened that no one in the weekend's excitement would remember except me. It has strongly affected me for the last fifty years. It gave me a "light bulb moment" that has haunted me for decades in a wonderful manner. It would burn in the back of my mind, and would be a motivating attitude factor that has helped me remain steadfast and determined in my own training habits to this day.

As was the custom in the tournaments of the day, we had frequent demonstrations of all sorts showing karate's awe-striking technical power; just to give the audiences a dose of healthy respect for this relatively new martial art form to the United States.

Sensei Dometrich had just stunned us all by breaking a round, 3-inch diameter, 6-foot long wooden pole with his shin using a front kick. Like most, I'm sure, I cringed thinking of my own shin bones shattered and flopping around as I watched.

He made it look so easy and then he calmly, and humbly retreated to the sidelines to watch his students in the next round of kumite matches. I was a new brown belt but wanted to be a life-time karate student. I did not care about rank, I just wanted to train. I was glued to the black belt kumite, when Sensei Dometrich came over near me. One of his black belts seemed to be very sharp and getting the upper hand in his match. I was enthralled! I leaned toward Dometrich Sensei and remarked how impressed I was with his breaking demonstration, and on how impressive I thought his Shodan was doing. I wanted to model myself after nearly every traditional karate black belt I could observe.

Sensei was so approachable and friendly. He thanked me for my kind words but then said, to my surprise, in thoughtful seriousness, "The only problem is that he'll probably quit soon."

What? "Sensei, I don't understand. He looks very talented." I was seriously confused.

"Well," he said, "it seems that as soon as people get black belt, they just quit. It's like they think they know everything about karate when they get to Shodan, so they quit. I haven't quite figured it out yet."

I was stunned. Few words said from Sensei, but a chill ran down my spine. I was a brown belt with Shodan moving into my sights, but I planned on doing karate, learning all I could, for my whole life. Quit after black belt? Never! I would just be getting started! I wanted to know everything I could learn, everything!

Being a good black belt, I thought, is to realize that there is just much, much more left to learn. Still the more I learn, the more I see that I just don't know. But if I were to quit, I would be quitting on myself most of all. Just at the threshold of fresh new insights, new paradigm shifts, and new knowledge of the karate world that could change my life, and the lives of my students, forever.

Osamu Ozawa once commented to us that "black belts who think they 'know it all' about karate think they are Big Shots!"

This logic seemed to me it would be much like swimming two-thirds of the way across the English Channel, and deciding you can't make it, so you quit, turn around, and swim back. Quitting as a black belt because there is nothing left to learn? Ludicrous!

I continued to follow his articles and columns over the years. I have repeated this story easily a hundred times since, to my own students. Once, without me knowing, my students wrote a letter to Sensei Dometrich, and told him I had been them telling this story, because it challenged us all to not quit at the threshold of new insight. When *The Endless Quest* was published, my students presented me with an autographed copy. Inside he wrote me a note of well wishes, and in his beautiful classic style he ended with, *"To the beginner there are many answers to a problem. To the expert there is only one, 'beginners mind'."*

That says an awful lot.

CHAPTER 36

The Never-Quitting Spirit, Funakoshi, Ozawa, Schmidt...

THE MASTERS IN ALL *BUDO* have impressed upon us the pitfalls of quitting. They really knew what they were talking about. Not the least, is that life and death may depend on it. The biggest loss is the life time of benefits that are missed. Clearly, they believed, and I think we are establishing, that karate-do gives a motivational driving life-force that affects positively many, many aspects of our lives. But everyone must make personal choices for themselves.

One of the highest karate compliments I was ever paid was from Sensei Edward Kuras when in a light moment of sharing karate war-stories, he laughed and said, "Rick, you're a lifer. You are a lifer, man!" Sensei Ed Kuras is a "lifer" in karate as well. He has taught and trained for over fifty years in his dojos and programs at Western Illinois University, and has been a USA Team coach for international competitions many times. If one accepts the "lifer" label in karate-do, quitting doesn't seem to be an option. It's a high honor.

In his biographic literature, you will find that Gichin Funakoshi himself felt the sting of losing students in WWII, dojos were wiped off the map, and is own son died of illness in his prime. But did he give up? No. Quite to the contrary, he seems to have transformed all disappointment and heart-ache into the determination to work even harder to teach his Japanese Karate until his last day.

In Osamu Ozawa Sensei's own words, in person and in his biography, written by Sensei Randall G. Hassell, time after time when he was at rock-bottom in his life, he would fight his way back up. One of my favorite stories of his, which he told me firsthand, was his WWII experience. After his plane crashed on take-off, he was injured and in traction when the radio in his hospital announced Japan's unconditional surrender. He was immobilized in traction, broken limbs, puncture lung, blown out ear drum and more. Hearing the announcement, he told us, suddenly patients all around him started committing suicide. He luckily (for thousands of karate students,) was tied and immobilized in casts and traction, too disabled to join them. Months later, he hobbled homeward to see if he could find his surviving family in the devastation of an atomic bomb. He said he came to a vacant lot where his home had been and found a note about the Ozawa family. He finally found them. They were so shocked to see him because, thinking he was dead, they had conducted his funeral several weeks earlier. He said when they opened the door and saw him, their eyes really got big; they were stunned. But did this stop Osamu Ozawa? Not at all. In fact, he with other karate masters to increase Shotokan's popularity in Japan and in later in the US.

He was both a pauper and a millionaire several times over, and he never gave up. If we measure our doubts about giving up "karate spirit-training" against the benchmarks set by predecessors like Osamu Ozawa.

I had written about the legendary Sensei Stan Schmidt in a couple magazine articles just after Sensei Schmidt had both hips replaced. He was at that time, the only non-Japanese to be on the Japan Karate Association's Shihankai (Board of Masters) in Japan. At the time, he had been promoted to 7th Dan by the JKA. His credentials continue to be extraordinarily impressive. But most impressive were the personal visits with him, as he worked with Sensei Hassell on publishing books and DVDs.

I even have the 1970s movie, *Kill and Kill Again*, which Sensei Schmidt appeared in. He played the "Fly," and he floated on air. Also in the film, Masahiko Tanaka taught a huge class from the top of a towering platform. On an average day Sensei Stan Schmidt is impressive—always inspiring.

However, even with all credentials and Hollywood magic aside, I was most impressed with his down-to-earth attitude. Before us was a karate sensei with two new artificial hips, long before artificial joints became common-place. His notable nickname in karate circles in Japan had been "Mr. Back Kick" for years. He inspired me so very much and I had no clue at the time that I would later get my own two artificial hips, as would several many of my peers. (But that's another story.) Sensei Schmidt told his story about being in the hospital recovering, and he was complaining about the pain one night, to his nurse, who said, "You are a karate guy, right? I thought you karate guys were supposed to be tough?"

Now, that comment, he said, was a wakeup call. That was when Sensei Schmidt found a rock that fit in the palm of his hand, and from then on, when he felt weak or in pain, he would punch the rock like a makiwara, Little by little, he would punch it with his knuckles to heal his spirit. Is this another excellent example of the true karate spirit? Absolutely. Did he quit? No. He never, ever gave up!

I want to close out this section on a personal note: I began training in 1968. I've been a regular guy training in Japanese karate the entire time and still happily do. Since I started, I've experienced graduating from college with a couple of degrees, military service, happily married over forty years, changed jobs a few times, been ill a few hundred times (as a career in education will cause), served on elected school boards and local offices, raised two kids with all the "happy" trials and tribulations that go with that territory. I had surgery on both knees, two hips replaced, and more. Could I, a regular guy, have quit training during any of those challenges? Of course! Did I? No.

I've had my own near-death experiences with major cancer surgery. This came as a sudden surprise out of nowhere. When I woke up and found out the surgery was successful, I knew it was "one bullet dodged" and felt better than if I had won the lottery. Once in the middle of the night, I couldn't sleep, so when no one was looking, I slipped out of bed and very carefully did Heian Shodan. I did it just for me. (This is a secret. Don't anyone tell my wife please.) My IV lines kept getting in the way, and I feared getting "busted" by a nurse, so I only gingerly did a couple. But it cheered me up beyond expectations: Spirit training! I would NOT recommend doing that to anyone.

I have always had a healthy fear of quitting just before I might gain some new insight, more enlightenment, a new lesson about karate and about life is always just behind the next door. I am competing only with myself and father time. I am spirit training.

CHAPTER 37

The Spirit of Peace through Strength

AS LONG AS SOCIETY'S WOLVES REMAIN HUNGRY, there will be the need for good people to employ greater forces to maintain peace and safety. Greater good and peaceful forces must hold the bad at bay to allow good people to live in peace.

Perpetual peace is a dream, at least for our lifetime. It seems that war is a natural human behavior that is triggered by large scale needs for resources, conflicting ideals, interests, politics, religions, and the like. Sadly, war is a large and small scale natural human behavior. Pressures build, conflicts start. Human conflict is as devastating and as natural as earthquakes, volcanoes, and tsunamis. Powerful imbalances build up until disaster strikes. In all cases there is considerable loss of life and collateral damage.

Likewise, pressures build for individuals and groups of people. At a YWCA where one of our dojos is, they have a nation-wide "Week Without Violence."

Where some people may wonder about a karate program fitting into that theme, we see it as a perfect fit. I love to promote karate quotes that quickly come to mind like: "All violence is bad," or "To win one hundred battles is not the highest skill. To win one hundred battles without fighting is the highest skill." And, "There is no first attack in karate." There are many more, but the point is easily made that "In karate, every week is a week without violence."

Most people abide by laws and just try to solve their day-to-day struggles, and avoid violence. However, we are the only animal species on the planet that works to hurt and kill each other for personal gain and greed. Sadly, some people have overpowering urges to disrupt society, break laws, and hurt their fellow human beings. Those are the people that we in karate train to protect our loved ones and ourselves from. We train to develop the physical power that, as Funakoshi put it, would "make wild beasts tremble," but at the same time, we train to be advocates of peace and harmony.

Karate as a beautiful martial art is a method of honing empty-hand combat skills and high-spirited defenses. Karate is also an extraordinary and practical way of promoting the spirit of peace. We train hard, hoping that we never have to use our physical skills. But our hardcore technique training combined with our proper spirit training is all about being a better human being.

Character and demeanor are in critical training as well in karate, we train hard to project peace. Karate character improvement involves conduct, ethics, and courtesy, honest, sincerity, and enthusiasm in meeting challenges to name a few. We train hard to strengthen our mind and body.

Karate-do is *budo* --- the warrior's way. Oddly enough, within the kanji for budo, there is a small character that means "stop fighting." Another paradox.

As we train in karate-do, contradictions slowly change to affirmations. The depth and breadth of true karate and the spirit of peace are apparent.

Reflections

The spirit of peace is not at all a contradiction with karate and other martial arts. But as long as the wolves remain hungry and prey on weaker people, there will always be the need for good people to employ an even greater force to maintain peace and safety. Greater force must hold bad forces at bay to allow good people to survive and live in peace.

Performing the *Heian* kata, named for "peace" in fact, in a high-spirited, concentrated and powerful manner, is symbolic. In fact, in the literature, Funakoshi said that if trained long and hard at the Heian kata, we have learned sufficient fighting skills to defend against most opponents.

Police officer James Hartman, is a Karate Godan, a police defensive tactics instructor, and firearms tactics instructor. His job is "to protect and serve." He takes that literally. He and other police officers put their lives in danger each day to keep peace and protect the rest of us. Hartman likes to teach Heian Shodan in the most traditional way, and then he adds his twist. He teaches Heian kata in a method he calls "fighting kata." Stressing that powerful technique could be a natural deterrent, he'll have students perform Heian Shodan doing every technique, attacking or blocking, as a full-speed attack. Putting students in the frame of mind of a last resort situation, they explosively perform every technique, blocks as well, as an attack. Since this is very familiar, basic, and often practiced kata it is easily understood. Students do it in a very different, fighting-spirited manner. The spirit of peaceful defensive study, but with inherent technical strength, is nurtured when normally training in Heian Shodan. Often when Hartman teaches kata as a "fighting" kata, he stresses that all movements in all directions are performed as attacks or counterattacks. Consequently, it is the same kata, but done in a different spirit to make it change from a classical Shotokan training kata to the feeling of all-out explosive combat training. The same kata, just a different feeling while training for strength, speed and aggressiveness. Then, when students learn other kata they tend to learn at deeper levels. Peace through strength.

CHAPTER 38

Miyamoto Musashi: The Sword Saint and his Spirit Training Journey

THE BEGINNER MAY WONDER what a sword master from over four hundred years ago writing scrolls in a cave has to with karate training. Miyamoto Musashi's reputation came from studying combat, usually, man to man, although he was known to have been in war conflict. He is often known as the "Sword Saint."

He shares his thoughts on combat strategy that he learned from a life-time of studying. He explained that strategy can be successfully applied to many vocations, as well as the martial arts. He stresses, no matter which translation you read, that his way of strategy is can be applied to life. Concepts from his book of strategy are "universal" and are valuable in most combat situations one way or another. Since he speaks from a position of winning some sixty duals and fights, using his cunning strategies, and his tactics and techniques resulting from obsessive training, study and reflection, the relevance to karate-do is self-evident. Just the fact that after all he had been through, to retire to his cave at the age of 60 to put his thoughts to brush, speaks volumes.

Miyamoto Musashi was born in about 1584 and died in 1645 after writing *Go Rin No Sho (The Book of Five rings)*. His travels and exploits are as famous as any warrior or celebrity in the history of Japan. Known mostly for excellence with swords, in his later years, when he felt he had truly mastered the way of strategy, he began dueling with wooden sticks, carved oars and other sorts of wooden weapons. He is famous for his use of two swords. His contention was that he was nearly invincible in the art of the strategy with the sword, and that he could therefore use anything, with his strategy and combat tactics, and win. It was at this point in his life, in his late 50s, that he retired to a cave to meditate and write *Go Rin No Sho*. Many translations of this book are widely sold today in any book store. And many more references to Musashi's strategies are used in many martial arts. Strategy is strategy whether there is a sword, other weapons or if the weapons are the bare hands and feet. Direct applications are quite easy to find and use.

Frequent references to his own "spirit training" are often noted casually in his rhetoric and could be overlooked by the beginner. As much as his tactics and strategies are his most noticeable topics, Musashi does not neglect his proper state of mind, his spirit and meshes them into his strategies. He often stresses the proper state of mind and the proper spirit that must accompany strategies and tactics.

Considering the importance of Musashi's influence on so many other martial art endeavors in Japan, it is essential to see what his thoughts on spirit training are. How does he utilize the potential power of the mind and body combined?

In addition to Musashi's book, a wonderful book you might like is *Musashi,* by Eiji Yoshikawa. According to Harvard professor and one-time ambassador to Japan, Edwin O. Reichaur, it first appeared between 1935-1939 in Japan's largest newspaper, the *Asahi Shimbun,* in serialized form. It is based on historically correct facts and events of a period of Musashi's life, and it has been in book form over 14 times, seven times in film, on stage, and in TV series at least three times. The author fills in the blanks to make you feel as if you are along for his adventures. It is an enjoyable read for any martial artist.

Let's explore the thoughts on spirit training from Miyamoto Musashi.

Book of Five Rings Insights

Musashi's *Book of Five Rings* is divided into five books: Ground (Earth), Water, Fire, Wind and Void (Emptiness). These are according to the strategies and tactics discussed in each section. Musashi's concepts often overlap from book to book according to the strategy, fight conditions, number of opponents, and more. My discussions here emphasize what I feel are his instructions and ideas that easily lend themselves to karate. A concept may, in fact, show up in multiple books. Remember that his spirit, his strategies, and his tactics are all based on going to the essence of greatest necessity—to win. No one has ever claimed to know what exactly was going on in his mind. He was a genius in field. But I think we can learn so much from studying, experimenting, and trying to apply ideas from what he has written to karate. I've been trying to do so for decades by experimenting and designing karate drills for my students. Often, with student successes, they are surprised and smile as they attack each other with the ferocity of lions. And of course, there are those many times when I get those "deer-in-headlight" looks that say, "Back to the drawing board." It's all good learning.

There can be no second place

Musashi comes from pretty much from one mindset: you will live, or you will die. Your strategies and training, and the quality or your commitment and being in the proper fighting spirit may determine that outcome.

Osamu Ozawa often stressed that whether in dojo training, or in tournament competition, we control our distance so that practice and competitions are safe. But, he stressed that our spirit should show the strong "intent to hit them!" That way, students know what it feels like to be faced with a terrifying aggressor if they must use karate to save their life on the street. Training is safe but intensely useful.

I was most intrigued long ago when I found Musashi's strategies, attitudes, and principles showing up in many karate texts. Then, the more I read and crossed referenced his ideas, the more I found karate training and Musashi's ideas intertwined. I went through the *Book of Five Rings* incessantly for years to convert his ideas to karate class drills I could use. As an instructor, it was just plain enjoyable.

This is important to train in karate with much the same mind-set; as life could be in the balance. It is helpful to study each concept that might relate to our karate training one at a time, thoughtfully, reflectively, and to study them deeply. Many things related to karate can be studied in *Go Rin No Sho* as well, large and small, wide and deep. If his material is just skimmed over, much is missed. Musashi compares being a *kensei* (sword master) to be a master carpenter. If a carpenter can read and understand all building plans, and if he has the knowledge of using all the tools to do all the jobs in building structures, then he can construct any building with calm, confident, and knowledgeable methods.

Musashi claims that by studying his way of strategy he also was able to learn many other skills like brush work, fine art painting and carving, and even the skills of carpentry. He valued life-long learning and applying his strategies to master many things. I have an interest in oil paintings and other fine art. One day, while I was thumbing through a large painting reference book, I ran into Musashi's ink painting of a "shrike on a twig." It's in many copies of *A Book of Five Rings,* as well. When you first see it, one would see a nice Asian ink painting of a cute little harmless birdy, resting on a long thin twig, probably singing a sweet tweeting melody. But if you do a little reading, it appears that a shrike is a very aggressive little fellow who sits placidly over still water. He sits motionless as part of the shoreline scenery watching patiently, He waits for a small dinner-sized fish to swim by and the he pounces fiercely to feed. That explains at least one reason for Musashi painting what could be a symbolic martial strategy painting: for him, it was an artistic study in strategy, patience, taking the initiative, and decisive commitment for survival, and probably more. He also painted doves. Go figure!

Musashi stresses that his spirit in learning strategies for his two-sword skills, once mastered, can be applied toward learning anything. He says once he has mastered way in strategies, it's like a master carpenter building, and he draws parallels to make his points. The master builder has prepared himself in all aspects of building techniques by studying all related things. Just like should be done in the martial arts. If big surprises show up, according to Musashi, he will have a "settled and confident spirit" to solve them, all because of his training. That brings to mind the phrase, "Success is when preparation meets opportunity."

Success: When Preparation Meets Opportunity

As carpenters can begin building with knowledge, tools, and strategies; and with an unperturbed spirit, calmly adjusting as changes are needed, accomplishing final goals. The same is true with sword fighting as well as with karate. Know all that is possible to know, train correctly day after day, and use strategies to guide you because of your accumulated and dedicated training. We don't become flustered by unsuspected twists and turns, but more calmly perceive threats and attacks, and accurately deal with what comes.

Chapter 39

Musashi's "Ground" and Karate-do

MUSASHI STRESSED THAT THE "WAY OF STRATEGY" can be used in many walks of life to succeed. Musashi describes in his *Ground* book the importance of his strategy in many other things; for the sake of focusing on a few examples that can apply to karate, those things I have experimented with successfully with my students will be my focus. I'm sure many other instructors have done the same examination of *Go Rin No Sho* and can improve on the small number samples I present here.

Musashi has a simple and powerful teaching strategy that he uses often in his scrolls and brushwork of *Book of Five Rings* that is very successful in today's education in all subjects. He uses it but doesn't draw attention to it. It's a great tool for karate instructors of course, and is found in primary, secondary and college teaching methods as well. Musashi uses carpentry and other professions to say the mainstream strategies work everywhere. This is one that is simple and powerful. If you are teaching any class and you want students to learn the main objective, whatever it is, do this. Tell them what you want them to learn the most. (Tell them what you are going to teach them.) Make it clear what you want them to get out of your lesson. Then, simply said, teach them what you want them to learn by engaging them physically and mentally in the lesson. Karate is wonderful for this because students see you demonstrating, then they physically try it, do it, and practice it. They are moving around physically, shouting, seeing, hearing; they are engaged. They are learning what you want them to learn, and probably more. Then after time is up and all is said and done, then tell them what you just taught them! (Review.) So the strategy for teaching a good lesson is: Tell them what you are going to teach them. Teach them. Then, tell them what you taught them. Easy to remember and a powerful tool.

One can work on karate attitudes, spirit, and technical training principles using Musashi's principles. His fighting strategies are particularly helpful in instances of one-on-one combat, free-sparring, etc. However, to do so, we cannot merely practice thinking about only our punches and kicks. Musashi says not to spend as much time on "trivial specifics," but that we must step back and study the rhythm and timing of our opponents, so we know when to apply those punches and kicks. Just practicing the techniques without understanding strategy of timing in using them will not lead to success. We can develop the best weapons with our body, arms, and legs, but if we are not in the right place at the right time they won't help. And as Musashi points out in his *Ground* book, one must study all related things, big and small, fast and slow, and learn to perceive intervals and other breaks in our opponents timing, so that we can capitalize on them to win or survive.

The instructor is the needle, and the student is the thread.

Learn from every sensei, every credible source, and every experience. Learn something from everyone. Remember, you are learning the same things that your instructor has learned from his or her earlier experiences and years of training. They are passing it along. Learning from karate experiences that more senior karateka have internalized is much different, much more enriched, because they have learned it from the ground up. Karate is learned layer by layer. Often compered to building a house. The foundation first, that must be solid, then board upon board, one nailed to the other, to the roof. As a result, seniors and senseis did not learn on a superficial level but much more deeply, so they are passing along a much great depth of knowledge in karate.

Fighting spirit burns to run your fighting machine. If you lack knowledge, training, experience, and other skill sets, then you are courting disaster. Giving energy to ignorance is still ignorance. If you train hard, study hard, internalize, become knowledgeable, remain alert, and act with a calm determined spirit, you can become a highly effective and dangerous karateka. Karate skills are learned at first, in the beginning, from instruction, then practiced and practiced until they are second nature, reflexive, so that the sum of your trained karate skill is built step by step from the ground up like the mighty pyramids.

Musashi discusses the importance of understanding the opponent's "rhythms" timing so that they can be used to an advantage. If we understand the opponents timing, we can break into flaws or breaks that we can take advantage of.

Four hundred years ago Musashi contemplated and wrote these down; They are universal in use of tactics between single opponents and large-scale conflict to this day.

From the first time we do partner kumite drills, we are learning to see timing opportunities in the timing of attacks to practice basic blocks and counters. In Musashi's words, so to speak, we have learned the timing of attacking the opponent's openings in timing. As we build on these skills in basic sparring, we learn to do them in free-sparring. Since the idea of learning the opponents "rhythm" is a common thread in karate kumite (and every other combative activity), this allows instructors to be creative in designing their own student-training exercises. Eventually, after much training, and just as Nakayama and every other karate master teaches, we gain freedom from thinking about what to do with your body and instinctively, unconsciously react. Relevant very nicely to karate, his discussions of understanding the opponent's rhythms and timing to find openings and weaknesses to take advantage of with establishing our own timing and strategies and tactics are quite valuable. As you study his explanations throughout *Go Rin No Sho* there are many wonderful gems that have been applied in karate for generations. He often advocates being aware of the opponent(s) rhythms, postures, movements, timing, and advocating the familiar idea: the best defense is a better offense.

CHAPTER 40

Musashi's Book of Water and Karate

COMPARING THE KARATE SPIRIT to Musashi's book of Water, we must always be able to adapt and overcome quickly. According to Musashi, water always assumes the shape of its container in a calm, determined manner, and then it can seize the initiative overwhelmingly. Ask anyone whose home is destroyed by flooding.

Imagine a canoe is pushed out on a pond in the evening, when it appears as calm as glass, with no wind, no rain, nothing but a beautiful sunset. This deceptively serene picture might turn suddenly challenging if we discover there was a two-inch hole under the seat. Oops!

Suddenly, this calm friendly pond is forcefully coming in to fill the inside shape of the boat. Try as we might to bail, it gets filled. The water now takes the shape of its new container; quietly, powerfully, simultaneously, relentlessly. The canoe fills and is overpowered by the water. The calm water power wins.

This is how strategy and spirit must adapt in fighting, according to Musashi. In this manner, the opponent will underestimate your power, and at first (like the "canoe skipper") not notice subtle changes and smooth adaptations until it is too late. You smoothly adapt and overcome.

Spirit, strategy and tactics must change exactly according to what "is" instead of what "seems" to be. It seemed like our canoe would offer a fun ride. Then, the water adapted to the hole; it found a weakness.

Awareness helps to see bad things ahead of time, and adapt to the situation in real time, exactly as the situation requires, and without hesitation, all the while keeping calm but forceful. The more we train, acquire familiarity, stay aware, and research all things possible, then the more calmly danger can be adapted to and faced correctly. The knowledge and the ability to assess and adapt are power.

Musashi also stressed, "Do not show your spirit at any time." (Our pond looked serene but had much hidden potential power.) Musashi would not settle with just one strategy because he is urging learning the appropriate "spirit" for each instant, accompanied by corresponding strategies and tactical situations. These are a couple of examples that can be used in actual training drills:

Too high of a spirit can be a weakness.

If you are too nervous or angry, or too highly strung or impetuous, this can be a weakness that allows you to be tricked with deception.

Too low of a spirit can be capitalized on as well, and you may be overwhelmed by an opponent.

If showing a "low spirit," that might show illness, poor mood, weakness, or a physical problem, we can be vulnerable. Watch National Geographic. The lions, cheetahs, and wolves always gang up on and attack the sickly, lagging, weak-spirited member of the herd first. If you have pets, it is sometimes hard to tell if they are sick or injured because not showing weakness is in their DNA. (People are animals, too.) If weakness is shown, bad guys will want to attack with their strength.

A survey of prison inmates whose crimes were assault-and-battery related indicated their ideal victims were, not surprisingly, those who were unaware of their own surroundings; window-shopping, heads down, women in lonesome, dark environments, people sitting in cars looking down at cell phones, etc.

Stan Schmidt told us of his own experience after his hip replacements in South Africa. It was at the time as apartheid was ending and things on the street could be unpredictable and dangerous. As he was limping and walking gingerly along, approaching a crosswalk, he was confronted by a couple of hoodlums who, seeing he looked weak, felt emboldened to make the weakened gentleman into their victim. He looked weak, they felt strong. But Sensei Schmidt assessed, adapted and overcame, reversing the situation. He diverted their attention from himself momentarily by pretending that he saw a friend far behind them. He called out, looking toward his imaginary friend. When they turned to look, he strolled behind them, and crossed the street toward other people and safety.

He diverted their awareness and took initiative to avoid a bad situation.

Using outward appearances and inward states of alertness for karate kumite or in tense potentially confrontational situations:

If physically active on the outside, remain calm but mentally alert on the inside. Do not outwardly relax the body muscles completely --- be ready. If you are calm and alert inside to perceive the unfolding reality, be ready to explode at an opportunity.

If relaxed outwardly, in kumite or even sitting somewhere minding your own business, this can project that you are less of a threat (like the weak animal in the herd.) Keep an inside awareness very, very alert. A relaxed body is easily seen and will tempt an opponent to also relax (underestimating you,) allowing you to pounce if necessary, and they are more open to an attack. Be alert for the right time to seize the initiative: whether that would mean escape or attack.

NOTE: However, if your body is relaxed and you are not alert, not mentally prepared, or "asleep at the wheel," when your opponent attacks, then you cannot play catch-up easily. It's too late to assess and adapt. Your canoe is sunk.

Chapter 41

Musashi's Book of Fire and Karate

IN HIS BOOK OF FIRE, Musashi stresses the feeling of a spirit being far bigger than you. He suggests training by making techniques always big rather than making them small. This gives you the ability to overcome not just one, but many attackers. More specifically, move in with a "calm inward spirit" but with the feeling of always crushing the enemy.

Think of how this can be translated into karate kata for example. The karate kata already simulates practicing against multiple attackers from different directions. When I first began training as a beginner, Shojiro Sugiyama told us to make techniques as big as we could to increase our range of motion, and that would increase our power and consequently the impact striking force of all our karate techniques. He cautioned us against what he called "closet kata," with small techniques that were weak. Small ranges of motion used in techniques that are designed for large ranges of motion to produce large amounts of kinetic energy, can create only a fraction of the potentially available forces.

After someone is a black belt level and well trained, they have command of their muscle contractions and expansions, breathing, etc., so they can execute the same techniques, faster and with a shorter range of motion, but are able to create equally deadly force. Their breathing, muscular contraction and expansion, body vibration, and technical abilities are well trained. But for the first efforts of learning to master techniques, maximum range of motion should be the rule to work toward.

Musashi's "Fire Spirit" conveys the feeling of crushing the opponent, or many opponents. We can practice kata, for example, in a mediocre manner, or we can practice it with a "fire in our belly," like we are fighting multiple attackers from different directions. If we practice in this manner, our mind and muscle-memory, our "fighting spirit" and our unconsciously performed technique will work if we really are under attack and need them.

After the age of 50 we lose about 5% of muscle strength every year if we don't do activities that stimulate continued muscular-skeletal growth in some activity or another. "If we don't use it, we use it!" So in my humble opinion, continuing karate-do, training and cross-training with karate and other karate augmenting activity, is a superb way to stay healthy. After I taught a very rowdy advanced class, some of my black belts said karate basics were "the fountain of youth." (That hasn't been verified scientifically.) So, there is something to be said for working toward maximizing all aspects of fighting techniques, in the biggest way possible especially in our younger days, so that as we age, our ranges of flexibility and skeletal strength continue to be better than "normal." Our karate techniques remain strong. We can still overcome opponents with "Shock and awe!"… with "fire".

This is about the feeling of a big "fighting spirit," whether for a small fight or for a big fight with many opponents. You will be just as dead in either if you do not win. Always try to make techniques bigger with enthusiasm, with the feeling of fighting many opponents if necessary.

Fire is just as hot, whether a small camp fire or a raging forest fire. Musashi's strategy works just as well today as ever.

The concepts in the Wind book deal with an open-minded spirit that is keenly interested in studying and learning what others can do. This is what I like to call a spirit of extreme curiosity as a life-long learning tool. Musashi says you should study yourself less and study others more. By being inquisitive about others, you can better judge the quality and effectiveness of your own skills. You can then better judge what you are up against. This inquisitive spirit causes you to be more calm and confident as a result of all that you learn from observing others. An inquisitive, lifelong learning spirit can be a valuable asset in other parts of your life as well. One of the most obvious quality traits of all the exceptional karate instructors I have ever met is that they all had an insatiable curiosity. It stands to reason. When you train, you crave learning and improving techniques. You constantly think about tactics and strategies. Even when most of your friends are daydreaming, they may be thinking of golf, fishing, sports, and the like. While you daydream, you will probably be thinking of *kata bunkai* or the perfect kumite attack. If you realize you have been doing this for decades, you are probably a karate lifetime learner, and that's a great thing!

CHAPTER 42

Musashi's "Book of Wind" and Karate

THE CONCEPTS IN THE "WIND BOOK" deal with an open-minded spirit that is keenly interested in studying and learning what others can do. This is what I like to call a spirit of extreme curiosity and it inspires life-long learning.

Musashi says to study ourselves less and to study others more. By being inquisitive about others, we can better judge the quality and effectiveness of our own skills. This gives us the knowledge to better judge what we may be up against. This inquisitive spirit helps us to be more calm and confident because of all that we learn from observing others. An inquisitive, lifelong learning spirit can be an asset in other parts of your life as well. One of the most obvious quality traits of all the exceptional karate instructors, or those who excel in most anything, is an insatiable curiosity. It stands to reason. When training in our martial art, we crave learning and improving techniques, tactics and strategies. During relaxing moments, don't be surprised if tactics and strategies creep into thoughts, It's like a recurring chess game in our mind; just a karate version. While your daydreams, you will probably be thinking of kata bunkai, or the perfecting your kumite. You may be a karate lifetime learner, and that's a great thing.

Chapter 43

Musashi's *Void* and Karate

THE DEFINITION OF *VOID* is something that has nothing; no beginning and no end and nothing inside. In between the "no beginning and no end," there is nothing; there is the void. Circular thinking isn't popular in the digital world, but this is karate; this is the martial arts. In the beginning, before you trained, you could easily understand that what you knew could be called a void. "I haven't trained, I know nothing about karate, so I am in a void stage."

Understand that there are many issues in karate that seem intangible until you see the results. You started in a clear "void" of karate by knowing nothing. Then, you practiced for years and years, learning and internalizing many things about karate, and now that you are at a very high stage of training, how could that be considered the new void? Easily.

Let's look at a simple and very small example to see how "something could be nothing." Let's look at a focused punch and an unfocused punch on a makiwara. Focus is a rather abstract idea at first. Hit the makiwara. One punch makes a nice whack on the board. One punch makes a noise sounding like "Ouch!" from the puncher. Even though the idea of focus is abstract to the beginner, they soon understand, the results are very concrete. One punch has the concept of focus, while one does not. The energy in the form of a shock wave transferred to the impact surface is invisible, but very real. At the exact time of impact when that energy is transferred from fist to target it suddenly is visible.

What is the void is the calm and quiet, as the body holds tremendous "potential" energy in reserve. Skills to create kinetic energy and destructive impact forces in an infinite number of ways, are at such a high stage, there is no beginning and no end to them. Your spirit is calm and confident. Internalized karate skills are natural after years and years of training. Skills can be used without thinking. Karate skills become embedded and natural as one were born with them. They can be used to respond to the rhythm and demands of any situation. No preparation and thought is needed, and responds to attack without thinking. This is Musashi's "void" as it relates to karate.

As Nakayama and others have described, skills are able to be used from no prior preparation or thought, because of long durations and obsessive training, reaching the point of Funakoshi's "internalization." This highest stage in karate, as described by masters Funakoshi, Nakayama, Nishiyama and others can be compared to Musashi's "Void." In these stages, after much, much training in karate, no certain fighting postures are necessary to immediately execute correct responses against aggression. Even you don't know what you will do, one can react appropriately without thinking or preparation wherever you may be, and whatever you might be doing. This is the void; something dramatic seems to come from nothing.

I've heard from many students over the years after they have had to defend against an attack that was totally unexpected. Especially in cases with black belts, they would often comment that they responded totally intuitively, without thinking about it. They often did not how they had responded until after the conflict was over. Much like reacting to avoid a car crash, not knowing it was coming, suddenly reacting without thinking, and if you get through it, you may not be quite sure how or why. And then you start shaking!

Funakoshi often said that there are no limitations in karate, no ending to training.

In terms of Musashi's *Book of Void*, you must train so much that your skills are internalized and completely natural. They arise spontaneously from the subconscious, and seemingly from nowhere.

In karate we have a symbolism about the "void" concept to illustrate to new students. We show them a white belt and say it represents starting with no karate skill. While they are white belts, if they get attacked, their mind goes blank, and they can't decide what technique to use. This gets them into trouble. Then, if they train seriously for a long time, they can learn, progress, and practice until they get a black belt. If they are inspired and dedicated to karate training, their black belt gets ragged and turns white, bringing them full circle to the spirit of the void, and their belt represents their training. As their ragged black belt turns white again, they also understand that there is so much more that they do not know. They will have the "beginners mind."

Now, as the black color turns to pale and white, they may get attacked as well. In drastic contrast now, they have endless karate skills internalized into their unbconscious mind and into the muscle memory of their body. If attacked now, however, their mind goes blank just as when they were wearing a white belt; they don't decide what techniques to use. The proper intuitive techniques and actions automatically spring out to respond to and neutralize the threat. In a natural manner, their innate skills get them out of trouble.

Masters Funakoshi, Nakayama, Nishiyama, and masters in other combative arts, activities, and other countless fields of study, taught that at extremely high skill levels, one may perform in a completely natural manner.

Epilogue

I HAVE TRIED TO GIVE INSIGHTS to "Karate Spirit Training" as fundamental components of karate that direct the intensity and the successful implementation of all karate-do activity. Spirit training is multifaceted. There is the calm, deliberately disciplined everyday spirit outlined in the *Dojo Kun* of Master Funakoshi. And, in contrast, there is the ever-aware, split-second, explosive, and subconscious-directed reaction to danger that would nullify even a ferocious animal. There is the peaceful spirit that Funakoshi stressed was the essence and, indeed, a major requirement for true karate. And there is the highest stage where so much accumulated training is internalized that the martial artist can react appropriately without any prior indication of danger, at any time or place. What all have in common is dedicated and proper disciplined training of the conscious and subconscious mind, coupled with internalized technical training. Spirit training provides a multitude of life-forces to stimulate and guide karate energies.

High-spirit training is not unique to karate. Every military branch instills exponential levels of enthusiasm, high-spirited patriotism, and comradeship. Professional and amateur athletic teams nurture spirit training because they know that if equally matched teams collide on the field, the one with the strongest individual and combined mental strength and enthusiasm will prevail. This brings us full circle to the contention that if two adversaries in are evenly matched, the mentally stronger will win. If excellent qualities of performance are required, then spirit training is essential.

Through proper training, new patterns of thinking and behavior are formed. But just as Funakoshi is quoted, *"Karate is like boiling water; without continuous heat, it will soon become cold,"* so it is that mental and physical strengths require continued disciplined training to remain viable.

A clearly focused mind is the best conduit to direct high-spirited energy that results in quite remarkable skill sets. Some come to karate practice just for the exercise, satisfying curiosity, wanting to lose a couple of pounds, and maybe to get the burn that signals a short-term stimulant to muscle growth. It is easy to see the clear contrast with the skilled karateka who trains with purpose, with clear-minded focus. The difference is remarkable. And in the event, that these two hypothetical examples are attacked violently, the results will differ considerably. Our karate-for-exercise person might, at best, squeak by with limited physical talent and some dumb luck. Our serious karate student who trains both mental and physical skill sets will be a much more competent and dangerous person for an attacker to deal with. This will be a victim that comes with consequences.

The beauty of training toward the many abilities in this book is that beyond karate, they will affect and improve other aspects of your life. Daily living, as it is for all of us, is an uphill struggle. We cannot merely occupy space and use up oxygen. Proactive effort is a must. If we are not proactive and seeking improvement, we will soon, no doubt, be acted upon. We would be a victim of complacency. Diligently training the body, mind and spirit can put us ahead of the curve, being prepared for all sorts of unexpected challenges.

> *"If you are not moving forward, then you are moving backward. Nothing stays the same."*

The spirit-training perspective is extremely healthy. Obstacles become challenges, and attitude takes on a positive and confident disposition. Remember the paradigm shift using the mountains earlier on. Some people see the mountain as a disappointing insurmountable blockade. Others, with a proper positive spirit, see a beautiful landscape and a fresh challenge to stimulate and invigorate — a place to feel alive. Mountain climbers are famous for a never-give-up, enthusiastic spirit. They often exemplify the spirit of Sir Edmund Hillary who, when asked, "Why do you want to climb a mountain?" replied, "Because, it is there."

Skeptics and detractors may insist that karate spirit training is abstract hocus pocus or a smoke and mirrors act. It is, in fact, extreme reality. The evidence is visible and the effects are profound.

Like electricity in lightning, or the wind in a hurricane, or the water in a Tsunami, spirit power is harnessed, directed and unleashed with extraordinary results.

Raising The Bar

Karate training is an endeavor that requires us to make honest judgments about our own progress, and then to begin self-motivated actions toward improvement. It is an exercise in facing our selves honestly. Dojos do not have mirrors to admire our own good looks. The mirrors are all about blunt honesty, good or bad, in our self-assessments. They are a helpful reality check. They neither flatter nor degrade. They just show what is.

After assessing weaknesses and recognizing strengths, it is the karate way to become energized and try initiatives to become better. We adapt forward thinking postures. In karate, even small accomplishments can come hard. While it is fine to be proud of those accomplishments, we can't sit down and be satisfied. We are challenged to do our best, we make our best effort, and then to raise our own bar higher as a new goal. I have simplified this to a fun challenge for kids, youth, and the like, and turned it into a catch phrase that I leave with them as we part ways. They can walk around school or work and repeat it to themselves. Often (in a bellowing voice), I'll leave them with the words, "Always try your best, to do your best!"

This is all a product of the "never-give-up spirit" of determination that is establish as our normal karate outlook. If motivated to raise our own bar, raise our own standards, heighten self-expectations, then we increase levels of achievement, becoming a little better each day. This is karate's never-give-up spirit. And "there are no limits."

"Does the man move the sword, or does the sword move the man?"

According to Master Nakayama, after years of training the body, mind, and spirit in all aspects of karate, techniques are applied without the need for thought. Training continues until it is impossible to tell where our technique begins and ends. Does it start with an aggressive movement from an opponent toward us, or does it start with the instant we recognize from the smallest twitch or impression that a threat is eminent? The answer is unknown because our defense is sparked at a subconscious level without conscious thought.

I've known many excellent competitors who, in kumite, did not even know that they attacked and scored until they were stopped by the referee. I've met well-trained karateka who were victims of foul play, who reacted without thinking to overpower an assailant. They react in a rather calm, yet explosive, high-spirited fashion without thinking; all their actions were a blur to them. This is crucial to successful self-defense because law enforcement tells us that the average attack scenario lasts only a couple of seconds; a couple of heartbeats determine the outcome. Karate intuitive training glues the initial recognition of danger to the actions taken. Knowing only the physical techniques without proper mental preparation allows fear and self-doubt to cloud the mind and to paralyze and slow down muscular actions. "Paralyzed with fear" is more than an expression. It can be a life-threatening reality. Training to the highest stage, where mind and body action are fused, creates successful survival skills.

Training the mind and body to their highest potential is incredibly real. Look no further than at the first responders trained in your own community.

I was recently in a hospital, quietly healing, boringly surfing the channels on my TV, when a "code blue" suddenly rang out over the PA system. Someone had collapsed, not in the ER, not in an operating room, but in the hospital cafeteria. The place exploded into action with nurses and doctors running from all directions to the victim. They converged in teams and instantly revived their new heart patient. Individuals with highly-honed skills reacted instantly from whatever they were doing, and converged to become a life-saving team.

Fire fighters, police, and ambulance personnel with years of experience train to levels where reactions are deeply trained and spontaneous as well. These responders deal with life and death as a daily norm to help us.

Military branches teach and stress spirit training to ingrain teamwork with instant and correctly performed fighting skills. They aspire to being "the best they can be," as a crucial member of a team, acting together as a unit, with highest stage precision. One fond memory of my own military training was in basic training in the first couple of days. We were ordered by our "friendly" Marine drill instructors to charge a hill, as if to charge the enemy, screaming at the top of our lungs all the way. The purpose was simply to train our fighting spirit. High-spirited effort and explosive enthusiasm were the purposes. After we charged up one hill, of course we charged down the next hill, and then up the next! We had no skills yet. But we had spirit training!

When karate-do becomes a lifestyle, it becomes natural. As karate training becomes an expression of who we are, it affects our behavior, thought processes, attitudes and actions, according to the high standards of *budo* --- the martial way. At this point of training, karate skills are even comfortable. Like Randall Hassell's spider spinning its web, not knowing why, just spinning and weaving because that's just what it does.

Of course, as we age, scar tissue stiffens in the cold, joints grind, and the soft tissues don't stretch like they used to. Spirit training becomes even more necessary, reviving our positive enthusiasm, coming to our aid, and charging our batteries. After all, getting older isn't for wimps!

Encouragement lies with a high-spirited disposition, exhilaration, determination --- a sense of purpose. Then, even pain does not have to have power over us. Accompanied by enthusiastic goals, pain is diminished, and with a superior motivation, it can become a friend to stimulate motivation even more.

Karate awareness is one of the most important mental skills anyone can learn for any arena of danger. Awareness is a mental state or skill that must be active when all others are on hold. The awareness button must be in the on position as close to 24 hours a day, seven days a week, as possible. We try to be aware of all that is around us, all the time. With our human frailties, this is realistically not even possible with the use of motion detectors and radar. But being aware of what is going on in our daily life, walking in the city, driving, cycling, or enjoying recreation is a no-brainer. Self-defense awareness is always self-protection training.

The makiwara is spirit training's anvil. The seasoned veteran, punching for example, will relax throughout the entire movement until the instant of contact, exhaling as they move almost effortlessly at blinding speed until the punch ends with that characteristic whack! Upon impact the muscle groups used will tense in the correct order, exhaling will suddenly stop, and the eyes bore through with the mental concentration of a laser. The beauty of the makiwara is that the more you relax, the harder you hit. The power of the punch is measured as a shockwave --- a bolt of energy. With accumulated internalized training on the punching post, if confronted with an attack, we have the mental and physical ability to launch a high speed, lethal counter attack in the blink of an eye.

Spirit Training causes, motivates and enables us to act with self-directed energies, to the degree of intensity that is determined by our inspired state of mind, and our ability to use human potential. In defining true karate, Funakoshi set our benchmarks, from a peaceful spirit adhering to karate-do guidelines with fighting spirit and technique that will make even "wild beasts tremble."

EPILOGUE

The beauty of karate is that it can be incorporated into our everyday lifestyle. It is just as important today as it ever was. Karate training may be just what is needed to cope with highly stressful lifestyles while staying mentally and physically healthy.

When the lights go out and the laws of civility break down, and the beasts truly get hungry, dedicated karate spirit and technical training can improve survivability. Make no mistake: karate is a warrior art that even to the present day, forges the individual into a peaceful, stronger, more aware, more capable, and productive human being.

SPIRIT TRAINING:

Strive with passion;

Keep your mind open;

Maintain lifelong learning;

Take initiative;

Train your spirit.

About The Author

RICK BREWER IS CURRENTLY a full-time karate instructor, writer, and artist. He regularly teaches classes and clinics in the Central Illinois Shotokan Karate Association and in the Central States Shotokan that he and Carl Hartter co-founded in the late 1980s. He began formal Shotokan karate training in 1968 while attending Illinois State University and has been continuously training and teaching traditional karate since then.

Brewer has a Bachelor's Degree in Education from Illinois State University and a Master's Degree in Education from the University of Illinois. He has dedicated five decades to training and teaching karate, improving karate teaching methods, and to developing other black belts into outstanding instructors. From the beginning, he has been directly involved in building, teaching, and assisting countless karate programs in universities, high schools, recreation centers, and commercial karate schools. Over the years, his students have competed in state, regional, national, and international venues including the Budokan in Japan.

For 35 years, he was a public high school teacher and the Department Head of Career and Technical Education at Pekin Community High School. Early on, he started the Pekin High

Karate Club. In addition, he wrote the text and taught one of the first accredited-for-graduation, School Board approved, Secondary Education Karate classes.

Under the banner of Central Illinois Shotokan Karate, and after receiving outstanding community support for his high school programs, he branched out to develop many other community-based karate programs for Boys and Girls Clubs, YWCAs, area recreation centers, and the like. These and other programs are active to this day.

In the late 1980s, he with the Central Illinois Shotokan Karate Association joined the American JKA Karate Association (AJKA) and he was on the original founding Board of Directors and Shihankai of Randall Hassell's American Shotokan Karate Alliance (ASKA). He is a 7th Dan in Shotokan karate.

Brewer's work ethics reflect his admiration for historic martial art masters. For example, Master Gichin Funakoshi was a school teacher, Shotokan master, calligrapher, and poet. And

About the Author

Myamoto Musashi is greatly admired for his warrior skills however, in addition to his notoriety as the "sword saint," Musashi is famous for his written reflections and for being a superb painter and sculptor, and his paintings and prose are found world-wide in art and literature publications. So, in addition to 50 years of karate training, Brewer enjoys writing articles, books, and columns. As a freelance writer, he has had dozens of articles published in SHOTOKAN KARATE MAGAZINE (SKM), AMERICAN PROFILES IN KARATE, SAMURAI MAGAZINE, KICK ILLUSTRATED, INSIDE KARATE, MARTIAL ARTS ILLUSTRATED, MASTERS MAGAZINE and others. Brewer currently does a regular "Karate Insight" column in Master's Magazine. He paints oil paintings in fine art, and does detailed sculptures in welded steel and wood. Many of his favorite subjects are related to karate: Rocky Mountain landscapes and Mt. Fuji in Japan, eagles in flight and Native American and Samurai warriors. He has presented major paintings, featuring Mount Fuji in Japan, to such world-renowned karate masters as Osamu Ozawa, Hirokazu Kanazawa, Stan Schmidt, and Randall Hassell.

Brewer was the Technical Editor/ Reviewer of *The Complete Idiots Guide to Karate* by Randall Hassell and Edmond Otis. He was featured doing an extensive DVD interview with Sensei Randall Hassell for the premier issue of Master's Magazine. And he has a DVD teaching "Distance and Timing" from the Shotokan Masters DVD series from Tamashi Press.

One of Brewer's personal favorite, old samurai quotes:

"Live each day as if your hair were raging with fire!"

APPENDIX

Glossary of Names

DOMETRICH, WILLIAM J. --- William Dometrich is the founder of the United States Chito-ryu Karate Federation, 8th Dan, and author of *The Endless Quest*, his autobiography. Dometrich started karate training in Japan, while in the U.S. Army stationed there in the occupation force after WWII. He studied under Ichiro Shirahama; who was a student of Tsuyoshi Chitose, the founder the Chito-Ryu style. Since then, Dometrich has trained and taught Chito-Ryu in the U.S. The author met Dometrich in the early 1970s at an Illinois State University tournament. Sensei Dometrich had just splintered a 2"x2"x6' board with his shin, calmly walked off of the floor as if he had just taken an evening stroll, and stood next to the author. It was the friendly conversation following that demonstration that has impacted the author to this day.

FUNAKOSHI, GICHIN --- Considered by many to be the "Father of Modern Karate-do." In Okinawa Funakoshi trained at karate daily from childhood to adulthood, while being a school teacher for 30 years. He formally introduced karate to mainland Japan. Critically helpful to karate's perpetual growth, Funakoshi created organized methods of teaching and refining karate-do, utilizing high-spirited intensive kata, basic technique, and self-defense training. He wisely utilized university clubs to establish respectable credibility for karate as he introduced his karate concepts to Japan. After WWII, Funakoshi and his students, including Nakayama and Nishiyama, founded the Japan Karate Association (JKA) and began the introduction of Shotokan karate to the world.

HARTMAN, JAMES --- James Hartman is a 6th Dan. Having started karate in the Pekin High School Karate Club in the 1970s he is nowadays an instructor, a program facilitator in Central Illinois Shotokan Karate in the Pekin-Peoria area, and a senior Central States Shotokan black belt. Hartman is a Shotokan Karate training veteran, seasoned competitor at local, state, national and international levels. He is a senior instructor and veteran of the former ASKA Black Belt Development Program. In addition, and for over 20 years, he has been a Self-Defense Tactics and Firearm Tactics Instructor in the Peoria, IL, Police Department. Hartman has also developed a "Fight Back" Self-Defense Program for women.

HARTTER, CARL --- With over 40 years of Shotokan Karate training, competition, and teaching experience, Carl Hartter is a 7th Dan, was Chief Instructor and Director of the Central Illinois Karate Association, in Bloomington, IL, co-founder of the Central Illinois Shotokan, Central States Shotokan, and served on the founding Board of Directors and Shihankai of Randall Hassell's American Shotokan Alliance (ASKA). He and his wife Elayne, 6th Dan, have also directed and taught programs at Illinois State University clubs as well. For decades now, the Hartters have directed karate classes at Illinois Wesleyan University that was one of first few accredited college karate programs in the U.S.

HASSELL, RANDALL G. --- Randall Hassell was the Chief Instructor and Founder of the American Shotokan Karate Alliance (ASKA), and Co-Founder and at the time of his passing, President of the American JKA Karate Association (AJKA). He proudly developed and conducted the ASKA and the ASKA Black Belt Development Program and instructed clinics, seminars, and classes for all ages, literally from coast to coast. He is the author of easily over two dozen books including: *Conversations with the Master: Masatoshi Nakayama, Shotokan Karate: Its History and Evolution, A Samurai Journey: Osamu Ozawa,* (co-author with Edmond Otis) or the *Complete Idiots Guide to Karate, Karate: Zen-Pen-Sword,* just to name a few. Randall Hassell wrote literally over one hundred articles on Karate-do. And, among others, he founded and operated Tamashi Publishing Co.

INGBER, LESTER, PHD --- As a Shotokan karate sensei, and a PhD in Physics, Lester Ingber wrote the book, *Karate Kinematics and Dynamics,* in 1981. He was the president of the Physical Studies Institute (PSI) in California. In 1968, Ingber wrote a thesis on the physical and mental principles involved in karate techniques. Dr. Ingber presented his thesis to the Japan Karate Association (JKA) and the All American Karate Federation (AAKF) and became the first Westerner to receive their instructor's degree. His thesis was published as *The Karate Instructor's Handbook* in 1976.

HIROKAZU, KANAZAWA --- Hirokazu Kanazawa was a student of Master Gichin Funakoshi and a graduate of Takushoku University. He was one of original famous JKA international champion competitors and a premier instructors of the Japan Karate Association. Kanazawa then became founder and President of the Shotokan Karate International (SKI), with dojos in over 60 countries world-wide.

MCGATH, WILLIAM (BILL) --- Bill McGath, Bloomington, IL was the author's first "sensei" (1958-1960), one who taught and inspired the author toward a life-time karate "quest." McGath was a burly Bloomington Fireman who taught karate and gave frequent lessons and breaking demonstrations during evening sessions in his back yard. He was in the U. S. Marines, and stationed in post-WWII Japan, where he studied karate and other martial arts before returning home.

MUSASHI, MIYAMOTO --- Musashi (1584-1634) is often referred to as "Kensei" or "Sword Saint" because he reportedly won 60 legendary duels to the death by the time he was in his early thirties. He was, for the most part, a master-less samurai who wandered about testing his skills against various kendo masters. Often unknown, Musashi was also a superior artist, painter and wood-carving sculptor, as well as swordsman. In his remaining years, Musashi retired to a cave to write his views and lessons on strategy in the form of his book, *Go Rin No Sho*

(Book of Five Rings). This book, among other things, is unique because it is written in the first person, with Musashi teaching the reader his thoughts on strategy for individual combat and war. *Go Rin No Sho* is every bit as valuable today as it is often useful and popular for strategies in business centers in Japan, and on Wall Street, just as it is in martial arts dojos and war. This author found Musashi's book, *Go Rin No Sho*, on Michigan Avenue, on Chicago, Illinois' "Gold Coast," in the business section of a book store, still providing the "competitive edge."

NAKAYAMA, MASATOSHI --- Master Nakayama (1913-1987) was a direct student of Gichin Funakoshi and after WWII became the Chief Instructor of the Japan Karate Association (JKA). He assisted Funakoshi in helping create the technical standards and curriculum so that the JKA was officially recognized by the Ministry of Education of Japan. Nakayama wrote many of the first and most authoritative texts on karate, including the *Best Karate* eleven volume set, and the famous and standard-setting, *Dynamic Karate*. Two other excellent resources for additional information about Nakayama are *Conversations with the Master: Masatoshi Nakayama*, by Randall Hassell, and *Karate Masters, Volume 1*, by Jose Fraguas.

NISHIYAMA, HIDETAKA --- Hidetaka Nishiyama was a direct student of Gichin Funakoshi starting in the early 1940s, and he is not at all hard to find even if you are viewing historic karate videos of the Funakoshi era. He was one of the leaders of the JKA and wrote *Karate: The Art of Empty-Hand Fighting*.

In 1961, Nishiyama moved to the United States where he formed the America Amateur Karate Federation (AAKF) and later founded the International Traditional Karate Federation (ITKF).

OTIS, EDMOND --- Edmond Otis is an internationally known instructor, competitor, coach, and judge. He is one of a handful of the most unique and extremely popular, inspiring, and motivating American instructors. His classes, like his *Essential Shotokan* DVD sets are rich with technical information. Otis is a licensed psychotherapist who presents and coaches groups, businesses and organizations on using martial arts principals to meet their corporate and individual needs. Edmond Otis was the Shihankai Chairman of the American Shotokan Karate Alliance (ASKA) and the chairman of the American JKA Karate Association (AJKA).

OZAWA, OSAMU --- Osamu Ozawa was the most senior Japanese karate master in the Western Hemisphere when he died in 1998. He was born in Kobe, Japan, and first trained in Wado-ryu. He often told us a wonderfully charming story about "starting karate because [he] was so terrible in baseball!" At age 17, attending Hosei University, he trained directly under Gichin Funakoshi. He passionately wanted to be a warrior and joined the Japanese Imperial Navy as a pilot. Crashing on takeoff and receiving critical injuries ended his war abruptly. Weeks later, arriving home, he found a flat barren landscape from a nuclear blast. Lying in the dirt was a splintered board with some barely readable directions to the survivors of the Ozawa family.

When Ozawa found his family they were shocked to see him. (He told us their eyes were very big!) They thought he was lost in the war and had held his funeral weeks before. Ozawa's amazing life showcased his incredibly positive attitude and belief in the real power of karate-do. He rose from ashes to be a millionaire and pauper many times. You can read it in his own words in the book, *A Samurai Journey: Osamu Ozawa*, by Randall Hassell.

QUINN, TED --- Ted Quinn is a 6th dan and a senior instructor in the Central Illinois Shotokan Karate Association and on the Shihankai of the Central States Shotokan. Quinn started karate training in 1976, in the Pekin High School karate club with sensei Rick Brewer in the Central Illinois Shotokan. After attaining Nidan in the U.S., he joined the Air Force and was stationed in Japan for over 12 years, training, competing and teaching in Japan Karate Association (JKA) classes. For his first six years in Japan, he trained at the Hoitsukan dojo in Tokyo and was invited to compete in the Budokan with the Japanese Defense Force's Karate Team. He earned his Sandan in Tokyo, and was even presented a tournament kata award by the Japanese Minister of Defense. He received recognition for being an "ambassador of friendship" between countries from his military superiors. His last 6 years in the air force were spent stationed at the Misawa Air Force base, where he trained and even taught JKA children's classes. He reads, writes, and speaks fluently in

Japanese. Often when teaching JKA children's classes, their eyes were as big as saucers to hear their American *"gaijin"* instructor shouting commands in their native language. Quinn is currently a senior Central States Shotokan Shihankai member who teaches and trains in Pekin Illinois. In fact, he is now an assistant teacher in the very Pekin High School where he started karate training over 40 years ago!

SCHMIDT, STAN --- Stan Schmidt earned the rank of 8th Dan from the Japan Karate Association (JKA) and was the first non-Japanese to be awarded the title of *Shihan* from the Japan Karate Association. Three of Schmidt's books, *Spirit of the Empty Hand, Recognition,* and *Meeting Myself: Beyond Spirit of the Empty Hand,* are clearly as inspiring as his clinics. When he came to teach ASKA clinics in St. Charles, MO, and in Central Illinois, he often told a story about using a stone for a "makiwara" as he lay in bed in the hospital with a double hip replacement. He said that in the first karate book he ever read, it said, "The karate man must train every day." And that as he lay in pain he remembered that book, so to distract himself from thinking about the pain, he would punch a rock. How can you not be inspired about such a karate instructor? His books and DVDs, with his stories of training with instructors like Nakayama, Enoeda, Tanaka, Sugiura, Kase, and the like, speak volumes!

SOHO, TAKUAN --- Takuan Soho lived between 1573-1645, and was a proponent of the *Rin-zai* Sect of *Zen.* He was famous for his clever, rather dry wit and his admirably strong character.

He has been reportedly a strong influence on Miyamoto Musashi in most of the literature and the Japanese movies about Musashi's life, trials and tribulations. Takuan, was known to be an abundant writer, gardener, poet, tea master, and artist and calligrapher. According to the literature and legend, he was both a friend and teacher to Musashi, who was a swordsman, artist, and *ronin* ("wave man" or "master-less samurai"). But according to literature and legend, Takuan was also a teacher to the Emperor and the Shogan. According to his own book, *The Unfettered Mind*, (translated by William Scott Wilson), Takuan was able to move freely from student to student, high or low classes, with ease; and he never became narcissistic over his fame.

SUGIYAMA, SHOJIRO --- Shojiro Sugiyama was born in Tokyo (Yotsuya), Japan in 1929. Before joining the Japan Karate Association in 1954, he had trained in two other karate styles. He came to the USA, to Chicago, Illinois, to teach for the JKA in 1963. Literally thousands of students, beginner and advanced, since that time have been introduced or enlightened by the training in Sugiyama Sensei's Midwest dojos. Whether taught by Sugiyama himself, or by the many honored guest instructors like Hidetaka Nishiyama, there are thousands of black belts and their students world-wide who are affected by his work. Clearly the editions of his books, *Karate, Synchronization of Body and Mind* and *25 Shotokan Kata* (in English, Spanish, and Japanese) are a training fixture in countless gym bags and dojo bookshelves. With the students, books, classes, and the lessons learned by all, you can easily see the contributions of Shojiro Sugiyama and his Great Lakes brand of JKA Karate.

TANAKA, MASAHIKO --- According to an article by Stan Schmidt, Tanaka originally went to Nihon University to study veterinarian medicine and forestry, and even envisioned owning a farm in South America. At the age of 20 a friend invited Tanaka to visit a karate class taught by Yaguchi Sensei. He was hooked! After college he was a Sandan and he wanted to become a student instructor at the Japan Karate Association. They refused him because of lack of funding to pay for student instructors, but they told him if he could support himself he could stay and train in the "Hornets' Nest".

He worked odd jobs from being a river man, literally balancing on moving logs in the water, to selling real-estate. He often credited his strong stances and powerful movements to being on the logs. As an example of mental tenacity, Tanaka entered the All-Japan JKA National Championships 12 times before winning. Then in 1975 went on to win the world title in Los Angeles, California. Of crucial importance to the theme of this book, and to all those reading it, in an interview with Jose Fraguas, Tanaka says, *"Karate training is a mirror of life, and the way you live your life must go hand in hand with the way you train."*

TZU, SUN --- Sun Tzu is probably most noted in modern times from *The Art of War*. It is clear that among the many Chinese classics read by Funakoshi and his peers that the work of Sun Tzu was included and was of great value. Clearly the Japanese military studied his work. Written more than 2000 years ago, around 500 B.C., the essays and works of Sun Tzu may have been the first time the intensive study of combat and war were verbalized and written down for future generations. Even Napoleon was purported to have studied Sun Tzu's work. One very interesting parallel for traditional martial artists and Budo, is that Sun Tzu stressed that just having the power and strength were not enough to win. He taught that intellect, morals and the quality of the use of strategic resources and methods were more important than raw might.

YABE, JAMES --- Even now, James Yabe's technique is jaw-dropping. In 1961 he was the first All-America Karate Tournament Champion in both Kumite and Kata. He continued to dominate the American Shotokan scene by winning again in 1962, 1963, 1966, and in 1967. He was a member of U.S. National Team at the 1970 WUKO Championship in Japan and the 1972 WUKO Championship in Paris. Since he began training in 1958, Yabe has trained with some of the most renowned karate masters in the United States and in Japan, and he is one of the most senior students of Hidetaka Nishiyama in the U.S. His technique is mesmerizing and his teaching abilities are exemplary. He spontaneously conveys his genuine passion and love for karate-do in every movement.

Appendix

Glossary of Terms

Basai Dai: "Basai Dai" means "To Penetrate a Fortress" and is an advanced kata that is also studied in different styles and in other forms under other names such as *Patsai* or *Passai*. In Shotokan karate, both *Basai Dai* and *Basai Sho* are taught. Basai Dai is characterized by strong techniques and hip rotations and it can be traced back to Master Itosu, one of Gichin Funakoshi's instructors.

Budo: In simplest form, "Bu" can mean "warrior" and "do" means "the way." *Bu* can also mean reconciliation, harmony, or to stop fighting. So additionally, Budo can mean "the way of being a peaceful warrior."

Bunkai: The meaning or application of the techniques in kata, and an excellent way to teach kata in a manner that is meaningful and more easily remembered is to study how the techniques are used.

Dan: A level of black belt.

Dojo: A school, room, or place that karate and other martial arts are studied. "Do" means "the way" and "jo" means "the place." Therefore, a dojo is the *place* where *the way* is studied.

Dojo Kun: Proper principles of attitude and conduct for all of those who train in a dojo. Funakoshi condensed many "ideals" into five, generally known as the "Dojo Kun" that are often posted in a dojo for students to read and practice. Sometimes they are announced at the beginning or end of karate classes in a formal ceremony.

Gi: A common term used for karate uniform.

Godan: Fifth degree or fifth level of black belt, or in *Heian Godan*, for example, it means the "fifth level of the Heian kata." "Go" means fifth and "dan" means level.

Go No Sen: "Seizing the initiative later." Generally speaking, it means to let the opponent attack, and then block and counter, seizing the initiative, after your opponent's tactics are exposed.

Hajime: To begin, as in the command *"Hajime!"*

Heian: The name given to the most often used, first five basic kata in Shotokan karate training. Heian means "peaceful." Kata "Heian Shodan" would mean "Peaceful kata-level one." Likewise, kata "Heian Godan" would mean "Peaceful kata number five," or level five. In other styles of karate-do, they are called *Pinan*.

Ichi: One.

Ippon: One full point.

Japan Self-Defense Force: Japanese military forces.

Kami: Divinity or godlike.

Kamikaze: "Kame" means "divine" and "kaze" means "wind." Therefore, *kamikaze* literally means "divine wind." *Kamikaze* was the name given to Japanese suicide pilots used and noted, especially toward the end of World War II.

Kanji: Japanese writing/calligraphy.

Karate: "Kara" means "empty" and "te" means "hand." Therefore, *karate* means *empty hand*. Karate is an unarmed Japanese martial art using parts of the body as weapons. There are many styles and organizations teaching quality traditional karate world-wide. Typically the whole body is used, combining the mind and the body, to perform punches, kicks, blocks, sweeps and throwing in a combined manner to defeat the opponent. At the same time in traditional styles of karate, students are required to build positive character traits, and demonstrate good citizenship.

Karate-do: "Karate" is "empty hand" and "do" means "way." *Karate-do* implies that one trains at karate for much more than sport, recreational hobby, or for mere exercise and entertainment. *Karate-do* means it is more of a combined physical and mental life-style that improves the way one might conduct him or herself.

Karateka: A karate student.

Katana: The long sword with a convex, one-edged blade, carried by *Samurai*. It was worn with its cutting edge up so that it could be quickly drawn and swiftly used.

Kata: Prearranged formal exercises, comprised of multiple techniques that allow the participant to improved karate skills without the need of a training partner. Kata allow students to practice techniques in combinations, and from different angles, as if to defend themselves from multiple attackers from different directions and scenarios.

Kensei: Teacher of the art of the sword.

Kiai: A high-spirited shout that accompanies karate techniques. Sometimes called a "spirit-shout," it is meant to startle the opponent and at the same time give the karate practitioner an extra shot of adrenalin, energy, and confidence. Physiologically a *kiai* is a sharp, short, very loud outburst of noise, combined with breathing exhalation that helps you use muscle groups more efficiently for more strength and power. Mentally it helps you to focus your energy into the task at hand.

Kihon: Basic karate technique.

Kohai: "Kohai" refers to another student who is "junior" to you in rank in the dojo.

Kumite: Sparring.

Kuzushi: To destabilize or crush the opponent's balance and posture.

Maii: Distance.

Makiwara: Traditional punching board or punching post used in karate training to practice timing, breathing, relaxation, and tension all at the same time. Frequent and correct use of the makiwara has been historically used to toughen striking points on hands, feet, and the like. The physical and audio feed-back helps you understand and obtain the correct feeling of a focused technique.

Mizu No Kokoro: "Mind like water" is the general translation. A very calm and still pond accurately reflects all that is around it with crystal clarity like a mirror. Likewise, a calm and uncluttered mind can more clearly perceive all information, even the slightest bit of disruption or movement that the five senses can take in. Much like if the same pond is blasted with wind and rain, if the mind is cluttered with thoughts of fear and doubt, it cannot efficiently process perceptions and information accurately and swiftly. In the event of life-threatening circumstances, mistakes and incorrect reactions can mean life or death. Therefore we train to remain calm in the face of challenging situations in the dojo, to improve the odds that we can do the same in real self-defense situations.

Mu: Empty; clear of anything; none. Example: mushin ("mu") means "no," "shin" means "mind," thus *Mushin* means "no mind," the equivalent of an unattached mind clear of cluttering thoughts.

Musashi: Full name, *Shinmen Musashi No Kami Fugiwara No Genshin*, but he was most commonly called *Miyamoto Musashi*. Miyamoto Musashi was born in the 1580s in Japan. He is best known as the "Sword Saint" of Japan. Being a *ronan* (masterless Samurai) for much of his life, he roamed for many years sharpening his skills by challenging many kendo schools. He is best known for winning over sixty duels before retiring to a cave in order to write his strategies and philosophy in *Go Rin No Sho*, or *Book of Five Rings*. His strategies appear nearly all Japanese martial arts since then, and are still popular and extremely relevant today.

Mushin: No mind. It refers to putting ones mind in a state of emptiness to be able to react swiftly and accurately to any threat. The mind is theoretically uncluttered with disruptive thoughts that would slow down reaction times. This way a trained individual's actions can come from the subconscious mind due to karate skill sets that are, as Master Gichin Funakoshi often said, "internalized."

Myo: Enlightenment gained from doing karate as a regular part of your life, so much incorporated into your lifestyle that you don't have to think about it.

Ni: Two.

Nukite: Spear-hand thrust.

"Oss!" or "Osu!": Greetings often used between two martial artists to show mutual respect. This response or greeting can be used to show respect before training with a partner, or to begin and end a training session. Generally speaking "*Osu!*" means to "persevere" and "push forward." It is an important response for students to give to instructors that shows that the student understands, and is going to try hard to give their best effort. *Oss!* is also given at the end of a class or session in "thanks" for gratitude for being given a lesson by the *sensei*.

Samurai: The word Samurai means "to serve." Samurai were the top ruling military social class in Japan for several hundred years. Samurai were tremendously loyal to one lord. Only samurai were allowed to carry two swords.

San: Three.

Sempai: Means "senior" in the relationship of age or ranking in the *sempai-kohai* (senior/junior) systems in traditional martial arts schools. The sempai/kohai system often utilizes ranks and colored belts to indicate the levels of achievement, proficiency of karate skill sets and knowledge. Even in the karate black belt levels, for example, there are graduated levels of competencies and achievement. Anyone higher than your current level or senior to you is your *sempai*.

Sen No Sen: To seize the initiative earlier.

Sensei: Teacher/instructor.

Shi: Four.

Shihan: Senior instructor that other instructors and black belts look up to for guidance, instruction and an example to follow.

Shihankai: A "board" or "organizational body" composed of "senior instructors" (*shihans*).

Shin: "Mind" or "heart."

Shodan: "First degree" black belt, or "first level" as used in kata *Heian Shodan*.

Shotokan: The traditional Japanese "karate style" developed, taught and promoted by Master Gichin Funakoshi and his students.

Tsuki No Kokoro: "Mind like the moon." *Tsuki No Kokoro* is getting your mind globally aware of everything from large down to the smallest detail. The moon shines down on everything equally; it misses nothing. This is how the mind should be in the presence of danger. It is a state of awareness that is wide and acute at the same time.

Tsunami: Tidal wave.

Yame: Stop.

Zen: Unattached mind set. Karate is often called "moving Zen" because of the flowing unattached mental states karateka strive to be in when training.

Bibliography

CLAYTON, B. D., PH.D. (2004). *Shotokan's Secret.* United States; Ohara Publications, Inc.

DRAEGER, D. F. (1973). *Classical Budo, Volume Two.* New York, N.Y.; Weatherhill, Incorporated.

ENOEDA, K., & MACK, C. J. (1974). *Shotokan Karate: Free Fighting Techniques.* London; Paul H. Crompton Ltd.

FUNAKOSHI, G. (1973). *Karate-Do Kyohan: The Master Text.* (T. Ohshima, Trans.). Tokyo, Japan; Kodansha Int'l., Ltd.

FUNAKOSHI, G. (1975). *Karate-Do: My Way of Life.* Tokyo, Japan; Kodansha International.

FUNAKOSHI, G. (1988). *Karate-Do Nyumon.* Tokyo: Kodansha International Ltd.

FUNAKOSHI, G. (1994). *To-Te Jitsu.* (S. Ichida, Trans.). Hamilton, Ontario, Canada: Masters Publication.
(Original work published 1922)

Funakoshi, G. (2003). *The Twenty Guiding Principles of Karate.* Tokyo, Japan; Kodansha International.

FUNAKOSHI, G. (2005). *Karate Do Kyohan.* (H. Suzuki-Johnston, Trans.). San Diego, CA; Neptune Publications.

HASSELL, R. G. (1983). *Conversations with the Master: Masatoshi Nakayama.* St. Louis, Missouri; Focus Publications.

HASSELL, R. G. (1984). *Shotokan Karate: Its History and Evolution.* St. Louis, Missouri; Focus Publications.

HASSELL, R. G. (1989). *The Karate Spirit.* St. Louis, Missouri; Focus Publications.

HASSELL, R. G. (1991). *Karate Ideals.* St. Louis, Missouri; Focus Publications.

HASSELL, R. G. (1991). *Karate Training Guide.* St. Louis, Missouri; Focus Publications.

HASSELL, R. G. (1993). *Zen Pen and Sword: The Karate Experience.* St. Louis, Missouri; Focus Publications.

HASSELL, R. G., & OTIS, E. (2000). *The Complete Idiot's Guide to Karate.* (R. L. Brewer, Ed.). Indianapolis, Indiana; Alpha Books, Macmillan USA, Inc.

KANAZAWA, H. (1982). *Shotokan Karate International Kata (Volume 2).* Japan; Author.

KANAZAWA, H. (2004). *Karate Fighting Techniques: The Complete Kumite.* Tokyo, Japan; Kodansha International.

MUSASHI, M. (1982). *A Book of Five Rings.* (V. Harris, Trans.). Woodstock, N.Y.; The Overlook Press.

NAKAYAMA, M. (1966). *Dynamic Karate.* Tokyo, Japan: Kodansha International Ltd.

NAKAYAMA, M., & DRAEGER, D. F. (1963). *Practical Karate 1.* Tokyo, Japan; Tuttle Publishing.

NAKAYAMA, M., & DRAEGER, D. F. (1964). *Practical Karate 4: Defense Against Armed Assailants.* Boston; Tuttle Publishing.

NICOL, C. W. (1975). *Moving Zen.* New York; Quill.

NISHIYAMA, H., & BROWN, R. C. (1959). *Karate: The Art of "Empty Hand" Fighting.* Tokyo, Japan; Charles E. Tuttle Company, Incorporated.

REILLY, R. L. (1985). *Complete Shotokan Karate.* Boston; Charles E. Tuttle Company, Inc.

SCHMIDT, S. (1984). *Spirit of the Empty Hand.* St. Louis, Missouri; Focus Publications.

SCHMIDT, S. (1985). *Recognition.* St. Louis, Missouri; Focus Publications.

SCHMIDT, S. (1997). *Meeting Myself: Beyond Spirit of the Empty Hand.* St. Louis, Missouri; Focus Publications.

SUGIYAMA, S. (1984). *25 Shoto-kan Kata.* United States; J. Toguri Mercantile Co.

SUZUKI, S. (1970). *Zen Mind, Beginner's Mind.* New York, N.Y.; Weatherhill, Inc.

TOKITSU, K. (N.D.). *Miyamoto Musashi: His Life and Writings* (S. C. Kohn, Trans.), Boston; Weatherhill.

TZU, S. (1963). *The Art of War* (S. B. Griffith, Trans.). London; Oxford University Press

www.ingramcontent.com/pod-product-compliance
Lightning Source LLC
Chambersburg PA
CBHW071305110526
44591CB00010B/787